MAMMA'S ITALIAN CLASSICS

MARY-LOUISE RAPPAZZO & STEFAN RAPPAZZO

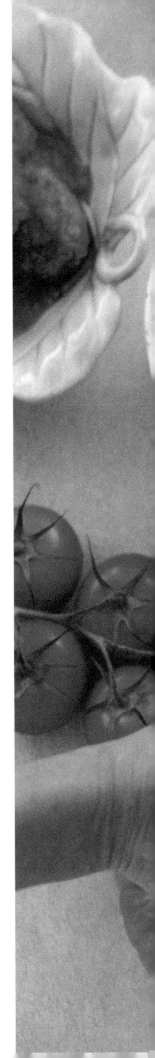

Book design and layout: Sadie Butterworth-Jones
Cover design: Raquel Buchbinder

Photography: Leigh Tynan, Maria Gagliardi,
Stefan Rappazzo, Mary-Louise Rappazzo

Paperback: 978-1-7778476-4-7
Hardback: 978-1-7778476-0-9
eBook: 978-1-7778476-1-6

CONTENTS

MAP OF INSPIRATION

MAP OF INSPIRATION

ASCOLI PICENO, LE MARCHE, ITALY

Mamma's birthplace and the point of reference to many of our culinary treasures. The region of Le Marche sits on the Adriatic coast between Emilia-Romagna to the North, Tuscany and Umbria to the west and Lazio and Abruzzo to the south.

The ancient city of Ascoli Piceno was founded by an Italic population, the Piceni, several centuries before Rome was even founded, hence the saying, "Ascoli era Ascoli quando Roma era pascoli" (Ascoli was Ascoli when Rome was still a pasture). With Roman ruins, medieval buildings and its Piazza del Popolo, in travertine and Renaissance splendour, Ascoli Piceno is a beautiful city, rich in the arts, gastronomy and strong traditions. It is a blend of ancient history and modern culture – truly a hidden gem.

We still have family in the region and we were lucky enough to have experienced the life and beauty of the city when we visited together, in 2014.

SANTA LUCIA DEL MELA, SICILY

Dad's birthplace, where Nonna learned to prepare traditional favourites from the Mediterranean, then brought her skills and knowledge to Canada and subsequently shared them with Mamma.

This small hilltop town is flanked by two rivers, situated in the province of Messina, where the boot of Italy meets the island of Sicily. The Aeolian islands are a daily reminder of the spectacular ocean views. Mount Etna's volcanic impact on the soil is a contributing factor to the rich and varied local vegetation.

TORONTO, CANADA

Ok fine... Hamilton / Burlington – the Golden Horseshoe of southern Ontario, surrounded by Lake Ontario, just west of Toronto, is the place where we grew up.

The city of Hamilton, the ambitious port city and leading industrial center of steel, is often referred to as "The Hammer", and is where Mamma and Pops both immigrated, with their prospective families. My parents met in Hamilton, married and soon after, moved to Burlington, a suburb and gateway to Toronto, where my siblings and I were raised.

Hamilton is divided by the Niagara escarpment, a large forested ridge, better known as the "mountain", dotted by many waterfalls and conservation areas. Today, Hamilton is emerging as a vibrant multi-faceted metropolis.

The region of southern Ontario has a prominent Italian presence, as reflected by the strong influence and cultural heritage imparted by the Italian-Canadians, in this area.

BUSAN, SOUTH KOREA

Yet another beach town! It is here, in the suburb of Haeundae Beach, where I lived and taught English, just after graduating from university, that I was first exposed to foreign culture. The language, socialization and, of course, the food, were like nothing I had ever before seen, nor tasted. It was an eye-opening experience that forged my path to perpetually wanting to live abroad, and to explore my realms of eating, cooking and appreciating different tastes and cultural norms.

I resourcefully acquired the ingredients to recreate many of Mamma's classics during my Korean residency and often cooked and shared meals with friends. On one occasion, when preparing an Italian meal for my Korean Hapkido master, I was begged, in order to appease his palette, to put kimchi next to his plate of spaghetti bolognese, as he could not fathom eating a meal without it.

GOLD COAST, AUSTRALIA

Australia's holiday capital, the Miami of Australia, is renowned for its nightlife, shopping, and mostly for its beaches. It's one of the great "surf cities" in the world, and annually hosts the first calendar event of the Pro Surfing tour. I lived here, just shy of a decade, initially, to earn a masters degree in education and to teach, but, after realizing that food was indeed my real passion, I put my teaching career on hold and jumped into the food biz. The popular nightlife helped to grow an impressive restaurant scene, and the accommodating year-round climate facilitated the onset of a thriving outdoor night market culture. One such market was the Miami Marketta, where I operated a mobile food stall, called Pazzo Panini, featuring many of Mamma's classics.

APOSENTILLO, NICARAGUA

North Pacific Nicaragua consists of a small cluster of coastal townships, sparsely inhabited, but with a rich landscape that fluctuates between wet and dry season. The coastline offers incredible surfing options, which makes the region a viable tourist draw being only 45 minutes from the closest proper city of Chinandega (to find a bank, gas station or supermarket). The national economy, at present, is in despair, but, despite the impoverished conditions of so many, the locals are some of the happiest people with whom I've co-existed. I opened a restaurant here, called "Pasta La Vista", where many of Mamma's recipes were featured, and where I enjoyed being part of an active and thriving community, until the civil crisis of 2018.

PARIS, FRANCE

I have lived in the French capital for the past three years and have enjoyed the work opportunities, friendships and family connections that it has offered me. It has also allowed me to be thoroughly immersed in travel and European food culture.

It was love that brought me to France, after I left Nicaragua, but now, after some time adapting to yet another new language and culture, it is love "for the city of love" that is keeping me here.

My experiences have enriched me in the knowledge of food and kitchen culture, and as a result, have led me to recently accept a new line of employment becoming a gelato maker and I am most excited to work for one of France's top Michelin chefs, under the tutelage of an Italian gelato expert.

Buon cibo. Buon vino. Buon amici.

Good food. Good wine. Good friends.

OUR STORY

STEF

Our cookbook project began in December of 2020. I came home from Paris amidst a Global Pandemic, and while reunited in lockdown, Mamma and I took the initiating steps towards making a dream come true. The truth is that this dream, for me, started years ago, when as a little meatball myself, I would watch my Mamma, in wonder, as she prepared some of the tastiest foods for our family to enjoy. In reality, however, the dream started generations ago, in the kitchens of my great-grandmothers (Bisnonne) and grandmothers (Nonne), who, in their natural elements, produced delicious, gastronomic meals, foods that would become traditional and be passed down to my mother and now to me. I came home from Paris to Covid lockdown in Toronto, and despite the fear and uncertainty of the time, or maybe because of it, Mamma and I decided that this would be the ideal time to compile and assemble our family's favourite recipes. We got to work – pulling out the old recipes, cooking, tasting, adjusting and polishing these beloved classics into culinary gems.

MAMMA

As a little girl growing up in the region of Le Marche, in Ascoli Piceno, I recall, with fond memories, images of my mother, aunts and grandmothers happily cooking and singing in the kitchen, while preparing, from scratch, everyday traditional meals. Once we immigrated to Canada, I saw my mother re-creating the same amazing Marchigiani dishes and thinking she was the best cook in the world. It made me realize how magical the art of food preparation can be and I knew that I would be following in her footsteps.

I spent a lot of time in the kitchen. My parents worked hard to make a living in Canada, so, as the oldest of four children, I took it upon myself, at an early age, to help out with much of the cooking, learning by necessity and attempting to keep up the old traditions.

Married, working and raising three children, I scurried around in the kitchen, cooking foods that I was familiar with, while also learning new ones from my husband's Sicilian background. My mother-in-law, Stefan's Nonna Filippa, was a typical Sicilian woman with high culinary standards of her own. Her approval was not easily granted and her signature response to almost anything was quite simply "No."

Soon, however, my attempts at Nonna Filippa's Sicilian meal re-creations were accepted and met with her approval of authenticity. I began to record the many treasured Sicilian recipes, adding them to my repertoire of Marchigiani favourites.

The authentic Marchigiani recipes were not so easy for me to acquire, either. My own mother, Angela, died before Stefan was even born, so much of what I learned about traditional regional dishes came by way of observation and osmosis, from my aunts and extended family. As the matriarch in our family, I made it my quest to carry on the family traditions, the way my mother would have done. Besides being an exceptional cook, Nonna Angela was creative, free-spirited and entrepreneurial, qualities that, today, I recognize in my nomadic son, Stefan.

STEF

From a young age, I remember family and friends finishing their post-meal compliments with suggestions for Mamma to one day "write a cookbook!" I loved the idea of it and often encouraged her over the years, hoping that someday it would come to fruition. I spent a lot of my time in the kitchen with Mamma, through high school, and regularly consulted with her before adopting her recipes to share with friends at university, and later with foreign friends throughout my global relocations.

With Mamma's aunts and uncles all living within a bocce ball's throw of one another in Hamilton, Ontario, Canada, I grew up totally immersed in these culturally rich culinary experiences. I looked forward to weekend-long food productions, filling deep freezers with trays of lasagna, arancini, stuffed olives and pesto, or making sausage and prosciutti, or producing the traditional high-volume sauce outputs that would fill family cantinas (cellars) with enough passata (tomato sauce) to last a season or two. Jarring fruits and vegetables, making pasta dough, pots of brodo (broth), and bulk assembly of all sorts of Italian classics was all just part of growing up as a little meatball.

My siblings and I would help Mamma with the pre-holiday grind when she would spend days preparing traditional goods for our family feasts, appeasing our ever-increasing

appetites, while always maintaining the quality control, not only of our late Nonne, but also of Mamma's insistent perfectionism.

So, it was a way to honour her craft, when I embarked on a series of business ventures, using her recipes as the backbone of my menus, first for my food truck (Pazzo Panini) in Australia's Gold Coast, and then in an Italian restaurant (Pasta La Vista) in Northern Nicaragua. Mamma's recipes travelled with me after graduating from university, as I relocated and lived in South Korea, Australia, Nicaragua, and now France. No matter where I have wandered, the quality and authenticity of these consistently and meticulously revised dishes have always been on point, and have proved themselves worthy time and time again.

MAMMA

Collaborating with Stefan on this project provided a deeper insight on the foods that we, as a family, enjoy and celebrate. Since many of the more complex and traditional recipes were initially recorded, "for my eyes only", I had to achieve a clearer understanding of my methods, in order to better explain them to someone else. As I wrote my version of a particular recipe, I could not help thinking that, from family to family or region to region, the same traditional dish can have many variations, whether in name, appearance, taste, proportion or in someone's use of a special secret ingredient, all of which provide individuality and authenticity in Italian cuisine.

Another realization is that with changing times, modern appliances and easier availability of products, preparing meals have become simpler and more versatile. Being adaptive to new influences, tastes, food allergies and restrictions, when preparing foods for the loved ones around our table, is an important factor to consider.

By integrating, rather than abandoning, old ways with modern methods, we can uphold and enjoy the family heirlooms, in particular, those included in this book, of which both Stefan and I are very proud to share with you.

Chapter 1
APPETIZERS

ZUCCHINI FRITTERS

yields: 16-18 .... time: 40mins ....

Light and fluffy on the inside, with a crisp and crunchy exterior, these healthy starters will keep adults, as well as little ones, coming back for more. Keep an extra batch in the freezer to enjoy as a snack!

INGREDIENTS

5 cups shredded zucchini
(about 4 small zucchini)

1 tsp salt

2 large eggs

1 garlic clove, minced

2 Tbsp finely chopped fresh basil

fresh ground pepper, to taste

½ cup grated parmesan

¾ cup all-purpose flour

1 tsp baking powder

3 - 4 Tbsp olive oil, per batch,
for frying

DIRECTIONS

Wash, dry and grate zucchini on the large-holed side of a box grater into a colander, set over a bowl. Sprinkle with salt, lightly toss and let stand for 10 minutes, to sweat out their juices.

Meanwhile, in a large bowl, add and mix together the eggs, minced garlic, basil, ground pepper, parmesan, flour and baking powder.

Press the shredded zucchini with your hands, to drain liquid, then wrap in a cheesecloth, twist and squeeze to release as much moisture as possible.

Add the zucchini to the other ingredients and combine.

Heat olive oil, in a frying pan, on medium-high heat.

Fry in batches. For each fritter, drop one or two heaping tablespoons of batter into the pan, gently flatten and cook 2 - 3 minutes on each side, until golden-brown and crispy. Reduce heat to medium if fritters darken too quickly before being thoroughly cooked. Drain on paper towels.

Serve right away or keep warm in a 200 F° (95 C°) oven for up to 30 minutes.

Serve with yogurt or sour cream, garnished with chopped scallions.

MAMMA'S TIPS

To freeze, layer cooled fritters between parchment paper and store in freezer bags. Thaw then reheat, in a preheated oven, at 375°F (190°C) for 10 minutes or until hot and crispy.

OLIVE ASCOLANE

yields: 80-90 .... time: 4-5hrs .... Advanced ....

Stuffed olives are a specialty of Ascoli Piceno, in Le Marche. The large pulpy olives are pitted, stuffed with a meat filling, and fried in a crisp breadcrumb coating. Delicious as an appetizer with your favourite wine, or as a side dish! They will test your knife paring skills, but are well worth the effort, even if you have to improvise to get that stuffing inside the olive.

EQUIPMENT

Meat Grinder

Deep Fry

STEP 1 INGREDIENTS

2 Tbsp olive oil

100 -150 g pork (shoulder, butt or blade)

100 -150 g beef (chuck or round)

300 - 400 g chicken breast, skin and bones in

1 shallot or half an onion, chopped

1 garlic clove, crushed

½ celery stalk, diced

½ carrot, diced

40 g pancetta, diced

salt and pepper, to taste

thin outer peel of ¼ lemon

1 bay leaf

sprig of 8 - 10 fresh rosemary leaves or ½ tsp dried

¼ tsp each ground cloves & nutmeg

½ cup white wine

½ cup diced or whole canned tomatoes

1 Tbsp fresh parsley, chopped

1 cup broth or water (or enough to cover ingredients in pot)

STEP 1 - COOKING THE MEAT

DIRECTIONS

Cut the meat and chicken into stewing-sized pieces. In a heavy pot, heat oil to medium-high and add the beef, pork and chicken; brown well on all sides, then transfer onto a dish.

Add onions, garlic, celery, carrot and pancetta and sauté, on medium heat, until softened (8 - 10 minutes). Return meat to pot, raise heat to medium-high, season with salt and pepper and add the lemon peel, bay leaf, rosemary, cloves and nutmeg. Pour in the wine, deglaze the pot and cook until evaporated.

Add tomatoes, parsley and enough broth or water to cover ingredients; bring to a boil then reduce heat to low.

Cover and simmer, for about an hour and a half or until meat is very tender and moist with some brothy liquid remaining.

When cooked, remove from heat and cool; discard bay leaf and any skin, fat or bones but keep the lemon peel.

STEF SAYS

Carving the pits out of the olives got you discouraged? Buy some pitted olives, cut them in half, make an oval of the filling, and adhere the olive halves to either side and continue.

STEP 2 INGREDIENTS

30 g of mortadella (optional)

2 eggs, lightly beaten

¼ tsp ground nutmeg

salt and pepper, to taste

¼ cup freshly grated parmesan

¼ cup dried breadcrumbs,
as needed

STEP 3 INGREDIENTS

80 - 90 jumbo green olives with
pits (2 large jars)

1 cup all-purpose flour,
for dredging olives

3 - 4 eggs, beaten

2 cups breadcrumbs, or as
needed for crumbing

1 L vegetable oil for deep-frying

lemon wedges for serving

STEP 2 – PREPARING THE FILLING

DIRECTIONS
Put the cooked meat, vegetables, lemon peel and mortadella (optional) through a food grinder. Strain any remaining liquid over the ground mixture.

Add eggs, season with ground nutmeg, salt and pepper and combine. Add the parmesan and mix to combine. Add the breadcrumbs in gradual amounts, as needed, to achieve a soft but binding consistency. Mix and blend well with a spatula.

Cover and refrigerate until ready to use.

STEP 3 – STUFFING THE OLIVES

DIRECTIONS
Drain, rinse several times and place the olives in a bowl of cold water.

Now for the challenge! With a small knife, pit each olive, by carefully cutting spirally around the pit and ending up with one pitless, coiled, whole olive. If the coil breaks, no worries – the pieces can be easily patched up! Keep the coiled olives in fresh water until all are pitted. When finished, carefully drain and pat dry the olives with paper towels.

Use the prepared filling to stuff the olive. Take a small amount of filling (a heaping teaspoon), shape into an oval, the size of the olive, then wrap the coiled olive around it. Smooth and reshape with hands; set on a tray. Use the broken olive pieces to wrap around the filling. Repeat until all the olives are stuffed.

Next, place the flour, beaten eggs and breadcrumbs, each in separate bowls. Coat the olives, first in flour, then egg, then breadcrumbs. Shape and bind well with the crumb coat and place on a parchment lined tray. Set aside for frying or freezing.

If freezing, place the olives on the parchment-lined tray and freeze; when frozen, transfer them into sealed freezer bags or containers until needed.

STEP 4 – FRYING THE OLIVES

DIRECTIONS
Heat the vegetable oil in a deep pot or fryer.

If fresh, deep-fry fresh, about 3 minutes or until golden brown and very crisp. Drain on paper towels. Serve hot, garnished with lemon wedges.

Deep-fry from frozen, about 8 minutes or thaw first, re-crumb lightly, if necessary, then fry for a lesser amount of time.

PICONI MARCHIGIANI

yields: 35-40 .... time: 1hr 30mins .... Advanced ....

These cheese-filled baked "mini volcanoes" are traditionally made at Easter time in the Le Marche region. They are delicious served with prosciutto, olives and other savoury foods, for brunch, a snack, or as part of your antipasto platter! Traditions aside, enjoy these cheesy dough-wrapped explosions anytime, warm or at room temperature, with your favourite glass of wine. They freeze very well.

EQUIPMENT

Pasta Machine

Pasta Cutter

STEP 1 INGREDIENTS

2 large eggs + 1 yolk
(reserve white)

½ tsp sugar

2 Tbsp olive oil

¼ cup water

1 ½ cups (210 g) "00" flour +
extra for kneading

STEP 2 INGREDIENTS

4 large eggs + 2 egg whites
(use the reserved white + 1 more)
(set aside the unused yolk)

150 g freshly grated pecorino
(aged)

150 g freshly grated fresh
parmesan

150 g semi-mature pecorino,
provoletta or scamorza,
shredded

½ tsp baking powder

½ tsp ground black pepper
(optional)

reserved egg yolk + 2 teaspoons
of lemon juice (or water),
for brushing, on top

STEP 1 - DOUGH

DIRECTIONS

In a bowl, whisk together eggs, egg yolk, sugar, oil and water.

Place flour in a heap on a board or work area, and make a well in the center.

Pour the egg mixture in the center of the well. With a fork, draw in the flour from the inner edges until it is fully incorporated with the egg.

Gather dough into a ball and, using extra flour, knead for about 10 minutes or until the dough is smooth, shiny, resilient and no longer sticky.

Place a few drops of oil on hands and rub on dough; cover in cellophane and refrigerate for 30 minutes to 1 hour.

While dough is resting, make the filling.

STEP 2 - FILLING

DIRECTIONS

In a mixing bowl, whisk the eggs & egg whites.

Combine the cheeses, baking powder and ground pepper and add to the egg mixture.

Mix well, with a spatula, to a smooth, firm consistency. Set aside.

CHEESY CHEESY
CHEESY CHEESY

STEP 3 – ASSEMBLY

DIRECTIONS

Remove dough from the refrigerator and set up a floured work area with the pasta machine.

Cut off a piece of dough (about the size of an English muffin), flatten and pat lightly with flour; run it through, once or twice, on the widest section of the pasta machine. Tighten the setting each time and continue stretching it through, until it is at the narrowest or at about #6 setting ("T-shirt" thin).

Place the stretched strip of dough onto a floured surface. Place a heaping spoonful of cheese filling, off-center, in a single row, a couple of finger-widths apart, along the dough strip. Fold the other half over, to cover the cheese filling. Stretch ends out, seal edges tightly and press out air bubbles by cupping hands around each of the piconi.

Shape into piconi (turnovers), using a fluted cutting wheel. Line piconi on a parchment lined baking tray, as they are shaped and cut. Repeat until all the dough and filling are used up. Scraps of dough, if not dried out, may be gathered, kneaded back into a ball and put through the pasta machine.

Preheat oven at 350°F (180°C).

Using scissors, snip the tops of each picone twice, in a cross shape.

Beat the reserved egg yolk with two teaspoons of lemon juice and brush the snipped tops of the piconi.

Bake for 20 - 25 minutes or until golden and filling ruptures the top, like a mini volcano.

EGGPLANT DIP

serves: 4-6 .... time: 1hr 40mins ....

Full-flavoured, fresh, and fibrous. Our dip is not only simple to make, it's also very nutritious. Delicious served with chips, crackers, pita or raw vegetable sticks.

EQUIPMENTS
Food Processor

INGREDIENTS

1 large or 2 medium eggplants, roasted whole

4 - 5 garlic cloves, roasted

¼ cup extra-virgin olive oil

3 - 4 Tbsp white wine vinegar

salt and pepper, to taste

¼ tsp cayenne, or to suit taste

8 - 10 fresh mint leaves, finely torn or chopped + 1 sprig for garnish

DIRECTIONS
Preheat oven to 350°F (180°C).

Wash, dry, and puncture eggplant, several times, with a knife. Place on rack, over a sheet of foil and roast for 40 - 50 minutes, or until eggplant is soft throughout when tested with a knife. Remove from oven and cool.

Snip ends off the garlic cloves but leave skins on; wrap in foil and roast for 30 minutes. Remove from oven, cool, remove skins and set aside.

Cut the eggplant in half and scrape the inside flesh (if heavy with seeds, remove some). With hands or cheesecloth, press and squeeze the excess liquid from the eggplant. Place the eggplant and garlic in a food processor and pulse just until combined (or place in a bowl and mash with a fork).

Add olive oil, wine vinegar, salt, pepper, cayenne and mint, in small amounts; taste for seasoning and adjust. Eggplant absorbs flavours, like a sponge, so it is important to keep adding and adjusting ingredients, to suit desired taste. Before serving, drizzle with good quality olive oil and garnish with a sprig of fresh mint.

Serve with carrot sticks, cucumber slices, celery or bell pepper strips, and/or crackers.

STEWED SICILIAN EGGPLANT
STEWED SICILIAN EGGPLANT
STEWED SICILIAN EGGPLANT

STEWED SICILIAN EGGPLANT
STEWED SICILIAN EGGPLANT
STEWED SICILIAN EGGPLANT

CAPONATA

serves: 4-6 .... time: 1hr 45mins ....

This classic Sicilian vegetable dish, with a hint of sweet and sour, highlights eggplants, onions and celery with texturizing flavour bites of capers, pine nuts and raisins. It's a great make-ahead dish that can be served hot or cold, as an appetizer over crusty bread, as a side with chicken or fish, or even as a sauce.

INGREDIENTS

1 firm eggplant (500 g), unpeeled, diced into 2 cm cubes

1 Tbsp salt, for sweating eggplant

½ cup olive oil, divided

1 medium white onion, thinly diced

2 small celery ribs, diced

1 cup canned diced tomatoes

½ cup water

15 (50 g) pitted green olives, halved

2 Tbsp capers, rinsed and drained

2 Tbsp golden raisins

2 Tbsp wine vinegar

2 tsp granulated sugar

salt & freshly ground pepper

chilli pepper flakes to taste

2 Tbsp pine nuts, lightly toasted

1 tsp unsweetened chocolate, grated (optional)

4 - 6 fresh basil leaves, torn or shredded

DIRECTIONS

Cube eggplant and place in a colander, over a bowl; sprinkle with salt, toss, weigh down with a plate and leave to draw out juices, for 30 minutes to 1 hour.

Toast pine nuts in a dry frying pan, on medium heat, tossing regularly, until golden, 5 - 6 minutes.

Rinse the salted eggplant cubes and pat-dry with a clean cloth.

In a large frying pan, heat ¼ cup of olive oil. When oil is hot, fry eggplant cubes, on medium-high heat, one batch at a time (adding more oil for each batch), until golden on all sides, 4 - 5 minutes. With a slotted spoon, transfer to drain on paper towels.

Alternatively, for a healthier option, toss eggplant cubes in about ¼ cup olive oil, season with salt and pepper, spread on a parchment-lined cookie sheet and bake, in a preheated oven, at 425°F (220°C), for about 30 - 35 minutes, turning them over occasionally, until cubes are golden colour.

In a large pan, heat 2 Tbsp olive oil and sauté onions and celery, over medium heat, until onions are soft and starting to caramelize, about 8 - 10 minutes.

Season with salt and pepper. Add the tomatoes and water, bring to a bubble and cook, on medium heat, for 5 minutes. Add the olives, capers, raisins, wine vinegar and sugar; stir and simmer, 4 - 5 minutes, until the sauce begins to thicken. Season, to taste, with salt, pepper and chilli pepper flakes. Add eggplant to the sauce, toss to combine the flavours, and simmer for another 2 - 3 minutes.

Sprinkle with pine nuts and the optional grated chocolate; stir to blend and remove from heat. Garnish with finely torn basil leaves.

For best flavour, let caponata sit at room temperature, for about an hour, before serving, or refrigerate overnight and serve cold or at room temperature.

CHEF'S NOTES

Chapter 2

SOUPS

ITALIAN EGG
DROP SOUP

ITALIAN EGG
DROP SOUP

STRACCIATELLA SOUP

serves: 6-8 .... **time: 20mins** (if broth is made) ....

Stracciatella or "rag soup" is named for the "shreds" of beaten egg that are dripped into the hot rich classic "brodo". Simple yet elegant, this flavourful soup is healthy, therapeutic and perfect any time. The addition of semolina flour or breadcrumbs serves to thicken and add body to the eggs but can be completely omitted, making it a delicious gluten-free dish. A great light starter for a festive meal!

INGREDIENTS

16 cups (4 L) homemade broth

8 eggs

1 cup grated parmesan

$\frac{1}{4}$ cup semolina flour or dried breadcrumbs (optional)

salt and pepper, to taste

$\frac{1}{2}$ tsp lemon zest

$\frac{1}{4}$ tsp ground nutmeg

DIRECTIONS

Refer to page 206 in the BASICS chapter for Classic Brodo recipe.

In a large pot, bring broth to a brisk rolling simmer. Season to taste.

Whisk eggs, grated parmesan, dried breadcrumbs, salt, pepper, lemon zest and nutmeg.

Add $\frac{1}{3}$ of the egg mixture to the broth, at a time, while whisking or stirring vigorously, in a single direction, to make shreds of eggs.

Let the soup return to a boil, in between each addition. Bring to a final boil and whisk to break up large clusters of eggs.

Ladle into soup bowls and serve with added parmesan.

MAMMA'S TIPS

Before adding the egg mixture, add pieces of cooked chicken (from broth), throw in 3 - 4 cups of shredded spinach or cook a cup of pastina in salted water, drain and add to brodo.

BARLEY & SAUSAGE MEATBALL SOUP

serves: 6-8   time: 1hr 30mins

A hearty and nutritious comfort soup. It's a complete meal that sticks to your ribs and makes for a very satisfying winter warmer.

INGREDIENTS

1 cup pearl barley, rinsed

4 cups water for par-cooking barley

4 links (500 g) Italian sausage, casing removed

4 Tbsp olive oil

1 medium onion, finely chopped

2 celery stalks, finely chopped

1 carrot, finely chopped

1 potato, peeled and diced

½ cup white wine

1 L beef broth

2 Tbsp tomato paste

4 - 5 cups water

½ tsp each of salt and pepper or to taste

¼ tsp each, or to taste, of dried thyme, sage, marjoram

¼ tsp chilli pepper flakes (optional)

200 g cremini mushrooms, sliced

200 g spinach leaves, washed, drained and roughly chopped

DIRECTIONS

In a saucepan, cover barley with 4 cups of water; cook, semi-covered, 25 - 30 minutes, over medium heat, stirring occasionally. When cooked, drain and set aside.

In the meantime, remove sausage meat from its casing, cut each link into 6 - 7 bite-sized pieces and shape into meatballs.

Chop and dice vegetables and set aside.

In a large pot, heat oil and brown meatballs on all sides, on medium-high heat, 3 - 4 minutes.

If pot is too crowded, remove meatballs with a slotted spoon and transfer to a dish.

Add onions and sauté, until softened, 3 - 5 minutes; add the diced celery, carrots and potatoes; stir and cook another 3 - 5 minutes until coated and combined. Return meatballs to pot.

Raise heat to high and add wine; deglaze pot and cook down until evaporated, 1 minute.

Add the par-cooked barley, broth, tomato paste and 4 cups of water. Season with salt, pepper, dried herbs and chilli pepper flakes. Bring to a boil, then cook, semi-covered, over medium heat, stirring occasionally, for about 30 - 35 minutes.

Add the mushrooms; stir, bring back to a boil and cook, semi-covered, another 20 minutes.

Add the chopped spinach; if soup is too thick, add another cup of water. Taste for seasoning and cook for 10 more minutes.

Serve with freshly grated cheese and crunchy bread.

SOUP
SOUP

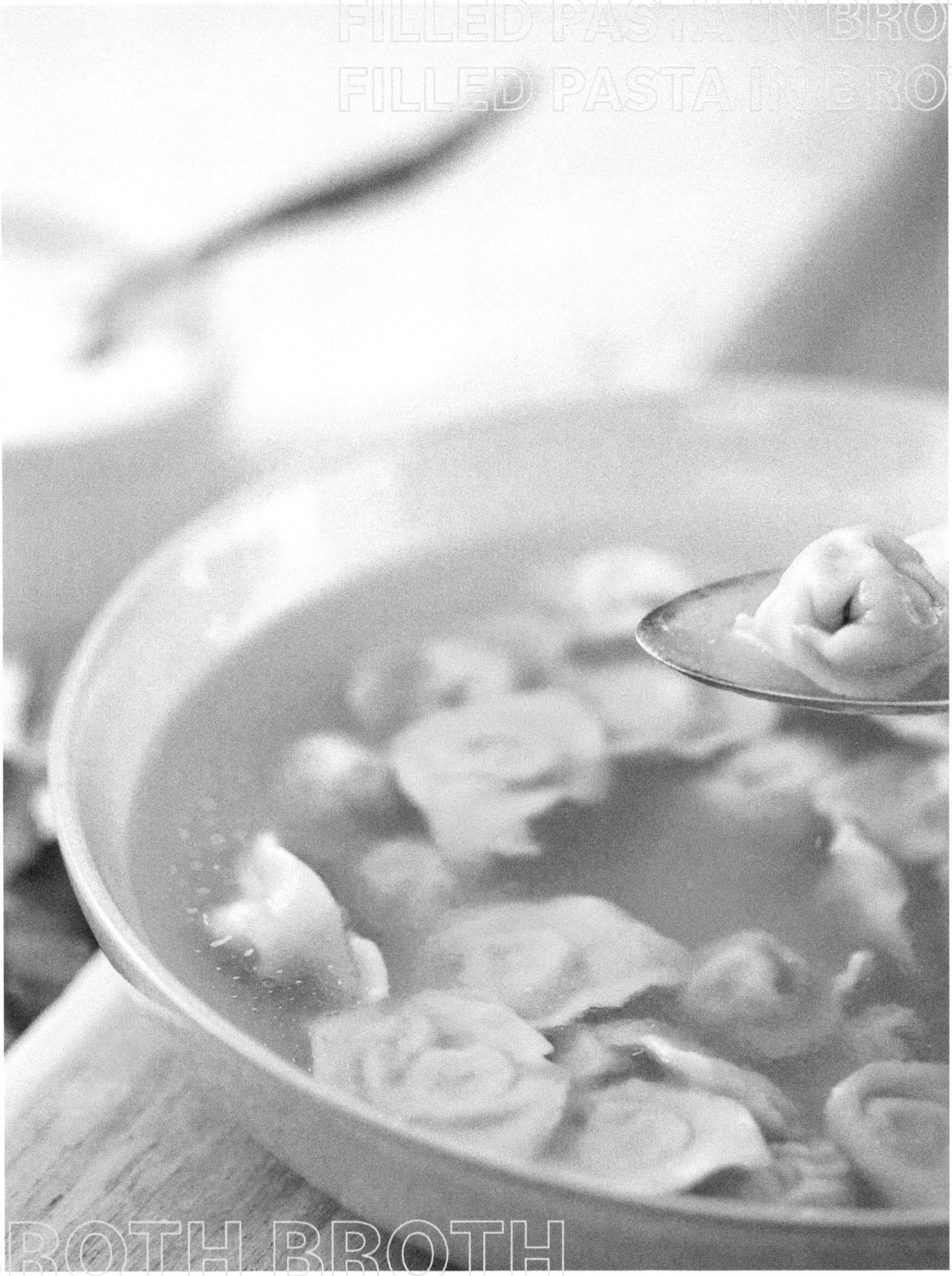

CAPPELLETTI IN BRODO

serves: 8-10 ·················· time: 6hrs ··················· Advanced ···············

An absolute classic! When you deconstruct the title, it's simple: "add cappelletti to heated broth (brodo)". But, when you break it down and start everything from scratch, the Italian way, it becomes an epic undertaking. Make a meat-spinach filling, a homemade broth, and fresh pasta dough (two basic recipes), then, stretch, fill and shape the dough into "little hats" or cappelletti. It's a labour of love and well rewarded. The filling will yield 320 - 340 cappelletti, with 20 - 25 per person considered to be a generous serving. Entice some helping hands, be patient and freeze the extra for another time. Enjoy the experience!

EQUIPMENT
Pasta Machine

Meat Grinder

STEP 2 INGREDIENTS
4 Tbsp olive oil

75 - 100g beef (chuck, round)

75 - 100g pork (shoulder butt, blade)

1 small chicken breast (300g) with skin and bones

1 small onion, roughly chopped

1 clove garlic, crushed

½ celery stalk (piece), largely diced

½ carrot, peeled and cut in chunks

½ cup white wine

salt and pepper, to taste

Skin of ¼ lemon (avoid bitter white flesh)

1 bay leaf

¼ tsp each of ground cloves, nutmeg, cinnamon

½ cup whole canned peeled tomatoes

STEP 1 – BRODO

DIRECTIONS
Refer to page 206 in the BASICS chapter for Brodo recipe.

The brodo (broth) can be made and refrigerated a day or two ahead of time.

STEP 2 – MEAT-SPINACH FILLING

The meat-spinach filling may also be made a day ahead.

DIRECTIONS
Cut the meat and chicken into stewing-sized pieces. In a heavy pot, heat oil to medium-high and add the beef, pork and chicken; brown well on all sides, then transfer onto a dish.

In the same pan, sauté onion and garlic, on medium heat until softened, 4 - 5 minutes.

Add celery and carrot pieces; cook to soften, another 2 - 3 minutes.

Raise heat to medium-high and return meat and chicken to pot. Add the lemon peel and season with salt, pepper, bay leaf, cloves, nutmeg and cinnamon.

Pour in the wine, deglaze the pot and cook until evaporated.

Add tomatoes, parsley and just enough water (about 1 cup) to cover the ingredients in the pot. Bring to a boil then reduce heat,

1 cup broth or water (or enough to cover ingredients in pot)

1 Tbsp roughly chopped parsley

200 g fresh spinach, blanched, strained, squeeze-dried;

2 eggs, beaten

2 Tbsp grated parmesan cheese

1 - 2 Tbsp dry breadcrumbs, as needed

cover and cook, over medium heat, for about an hour and a half or until the meat is tender and some brothy sauce remains.

Meanwhile, blanch the spinach in boiling salted water for about 30 seconds, remove from heat, drain and run cold water over it, to stop the cooking process. Strain excess liquid, squeeze-dry and set aside.

When the meat has cooked, remove from heat and let mixture cool. Discard bay leaves, skins, fat and bones.

Run everything else, including the lemon peel and the cooked, strained spinach, through the meat grinder, into a large bowl.

Strain any cooking liquid remaining in the pot, and add to the ground mixture.

Add beaten eggs to the meat mixture. Mix and combine. Add the grated parmesan; add the breadcrumbs, 1 Tbsp at a time, as needed, to achieve a "spreadable-like" consistency. Taste for seasoning. Cover and refrigerate until ready to use.

STEP 3 - DOUGH AND CAPPELLETTI

DIRECTIONS

Refer to page 193-194 in the BASICS chapter for Pasta Dough recipe for 12 - 16 (in order to use up all the filling).

Make the pasta dough according to directions. Cover, refrigerate and let rest for at least 30 minutes.

When ready to assemble, remove the prepared meat-spinach filling and dough from the refrigerator; prepare a floured work area and trays for making and placing the cappelletti.

While making the cappelletti, keep the unused dough well-covered, to prevent it from drying out. Run only one dough strip (75 - 80 g of dough), at a time, through the pasta machine, to about #5 or #6 setting – the dough should have enough substance to hold the filling. Set the stretched pasta sheet on a well-floured surface. Cut the strip into approx. 5 cm squares (or circles).

Place 1 tsp of filling on each square, fold the dough over to make a triangle; seal tightly, pressing around the edges, to prevent it from opening during cooking. With the point of the triangle facing you, move the two ends away from you and cross them until they meet; press the two ends together firmly; fold back the third point up to shape the "small hat" or cappelleto.

Place the completed cappelletti on a well-floured tray until all are done.

Use right away or freeze on tray, then store in baggies, until needed.

STEP 4 – COOK AND SERVE

DIRECTIONS

Bring a large pot of broth to a boil, estimating 2 cups of broth per person. Taste for seasoning.

Add the cappelletti (about 20 - 25 per person) and cook until they rise to the surface (3 - 4 minutes).

Use a slotted spoon to divide the cappelletti among the soup bowls then ladle enough broth over each serving.

Top with freshly grated parmesan and enjoy.

BRODETTO DI PESCE

serves: 6-8 .... time: 1 hr + prep time (up to 1 hr) ....

An authentic Italian fisherman stew with Adriatic influences, this elegant "brodetto" is delicious, healthy and packed with flavour. Follow our rendition or mix n' match with your favourite seafood, shellfish and white fish combo. Serve with crusty bread and enjoy with your favourite white wine.

INGREDIENTS

¼ cup olive oil

4 garlic cloves, crushed

½ tsp chilli pepper flakes or fresh peperoncino, seeded and finely chopped

1 small onion, finely chopped

2 celery sticks, diced

½ fennel bulb, diced

1 cup white wine

2 bay leaves

½ tsp dried oregano or 1 tsp fresh

1 (240 ml) bottle clam juice

1½ - 2 cups seafood or vegetable broth

3 cups (800 ml) canned diced tomatoes or fresh tomatoes, skinned, seeded and chopped

sea salt and ground pepper, to taste

500 g mussels, scrubbed and debearded

500 g fresh clams

500 g squid, cleaned, sliced into rings, tentacles halved lengthwise

500 g large raw shrimp, deveined, shells removed

500 g scallops

500 g firm white fish fillets such as halibut, cod, mackerel, snapper (choose one type), cut into serving size pieces

1 Tbsp fresh parsley and/or fresh basil, finely chopped

zest of half a lemon

3 - 4 Tbsp good quality olive oil, for drizzling

DIRECTIONS

Scrub and debeard mussels and soak in cold water for about 40 minutes, changing water at least once.

Soak clams in cold water for about 40 minutes, changing the water at least once.

Clean and prepare all other fish and shellfish and keep cold until needed.

Heat oil, in a heavy pot, over medium heat, and cook garlic and hot chilli flakes until fragrant but not browned, 1 minute.

Add onions, celery and fennel and sauté until vegetables have softened, 8 - 10 minutes.

Increase heat to medium-high and add wine; cook for 1 minute and allow to reduce slightly. Add bay leaves and oregano.

Add the clam juice, 1½ cups of broth and the tomatoes; bring to a boil. Season with salt and pepper.

Reduce heat to medium and cook, uncovered, until slightly thickened and reduced, 20 - 25 minutes.

Add clams and mussels; cover and cook for 2 minutes, until shells open up.

Add squid, shrimp and scallops. Mix to combine. If needed, add remaining ½ cup of broth.

Carefully arrange the white fish on top of the brodetto; ladle some sauce over the fish, cover and cook on medium heat for about 6 - 8 minutes.

Remove from heat; discard any clams or mussels that did not open. Garnish with parsley or basil and lemon zest.

Ladle brodetto in large soup bowls, drizzle with olive oil, and serve with toasted baguette slices.

CHEF'S NOTES

Chapter 3
VEGETABLES

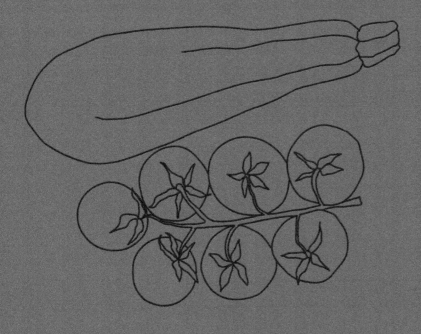

GONDOLETTE D
ZUCCHINI RIPIEN

ZUCCHINI GONDOLAS

serves: 4-8 .... time: 40mins ....

Reminiscent of the canals of Venice, these gondola gourds make for great mains, sides, or appetizers. They'll complement any protein and will spruce up a carb-heavy rice or pasta dish too. Quick and easy to make, these courgette vessels are bound to float the corners of your lips into a satisfied smile.

INGREDIENTS

4 small to medium zucchini

1 cup soft bread crumbs
(2 slices white bread, crust removed)

salt and pepper, to taste

dash of paprika

1 Tbsp fresh chopped parsley

¼ cup melted butter or olive oil

½ cup swiss, gruyere or fontina cheese, shredded

2 Tbsp grated parmesan

DIRECTIONS

Bring salted water to a boil and blanch whole zucchini, 3 – 4 minutes. Drain and splash with cold water to prevent further cooking. Snip off ends and cut in half, lengthwise. Use a spoon to scoop out the centers, being careful not to puncture the bottoms and leaving a rim of zucchini flesh along the sides. Discard any heavily seeded parts and keep the scooped-out pulp; squeeze-dry and finely chop or pulse; pat-dry the scooped out zucchini shells.

To make the soft crumbs, remove the crust, tear the bread into pieces and chop up finely, or pulse coarsely, in the processor.

Combine the zucchini pulp, soft crumbs, melted butter or olive oil, salt, pepper, paprika, parsley and shredded cheese.

Preheat the oven to 350°F (180°C).

Place zucchini halves in a greased baking dish and generously spoon mixture into zucchini boats. Sprinkle with parmesan.

Bake for 20 minutes, then broil for 1 - 2 minutes additionally, until the tops are golden and crispy.

STUFFED ARTICHOKES

serves: 6 .... time: 2hrs ....

Whether enjoyed as an appetizer, side dish or main, this aromatic thistle-like perennial is as delectable, in taste as it is impressive, in appearance. A labour of love to make, but fun to eat and every tasty bite makes it worth the effort.

EQUIPMENT

Steaming Pot

INGREDIENTS

6 medium to large artichokes

1 bowl of water

grated zest and juice of 1 lemon

4 cups fresh breadcrumbs
(pulsed crustless bread)

¼ cup grated romano or
parmesan + ¼ cup for tops

1 anchovy fillet or 1 tsp anchovy
paste (optional)

2 garlic cloves, finely chopped
or crushed

2 tsp finely chopped mint leaves

2 Tbsp finely chopped parsley

6 Tbsp olive oil + more
for drizzling

STEP 1 – CLEAN THE ARTICHOKES

DIRECTIONS

Zest one lemon; place the zest in a medium bowl, for later.

Squeeze the juice of the zested lemon into a large bowl of water, (along with the squeezed lemon halves).

Cut and discard the top quarter of the artichoke; cut the stem off at the base, but do not discard (the stem is very sweet and will be used in the stuffing); remove their tough outer layer with a knife, then place the trimmed stems in the bowl of lemon water.

Snap off the lower dark outer leaves of the artichoke and with scissors, snip the spiny tips of the remaining outer leaves. Open the artichokes slightly, by spreading the leaves apart to expose the inner crown of pointy fibres covering the choke. With a melon scooper or tip of a small spoon, scrape out the entire cavity and remove the pointy fibres and white hairy choke.

Place each cleaned artichoke, in the bowl of acidulated lemon water, to prevent browning.

STEP 2 – STEAM OR BLANCH ARTICHOKES

DIRECTIONS

If steaming: add some water to a steaming pot, cover and bring to a boil; reduce heat to a simmer. Place the artichokes, upside-down and the stems, in the steamer basket; cover and steam for 10 - 15 minutes.

If blanching; in a large pot, bring water to a boil; reduce heat, add artichokes and stems, cover and blanch for about 10 minutes; drain, rinse quickly in cold water and set upside down on a rack or towel, to drain.

MAMMA'S TIPS

Instead of baking, cook covered on stove-top over medium-low heat for about 1 hour.

½ tsp chili pepper flakes or to taste
salt & freshly ground pepper
¾ - 1 cup broth or water
½ cup white wine

STEP 3 – PREPARE STUFFING

DIRECTIONS

Make crumbs by pulsing the crustless bread slices in a food processor; place crumbs in the bowl with the lemon zest; add the grated parmesan.

Finely chop the steamed or blanched stems, the anchovy fillet, garlic cloves, mint and parsley; add to crumbs and mix to combine.

Heat oil in a frying pan, on medium-high heat. Add the bread mixture; add the chilli pepper flakes, season with salt and pepper and cook and stir until lightly browned, 4 - 5 minutes.

Remove from heat and set aside.

Preheat oven to 375°F (190°C).

STEP 4 – STUFF AND COOK

DIRECTIONS

Open artichokes by spreading out the leaves; fill the cavity and in between the leaves with the stuffing; fill loosely but to maximum capacity – the more stuffing, the better.

Place each filled artichoke in a dutch oven or deep baking dish, large enough to hold the artichokes tightly. Carefully pour the wine and broth (or water) around the artichokes, enough to fill the baking dish to a depth ⅓⅓ full.

Drizzle some olive oil over each artichoke and sprinkle with more grated cheese. Cover with aluminum foil and bake for 50 - 60 minutes or until the bottoms of the artichokes can be pierced easily with a fork.

Uncover and continue baking another 15 minutes or until the tops are golden.

HOW TO EAT

Have plenty of napkins and an extra plate for the petals. With your teeth, scrape the soft, pulpy inner part of each petal along with the stuffing, then discard the tough part. When you reach the soft artichoke heart, you can enjoy it completely.

MAMMA'S TIPS

Stuff, cover and refrigerate artichokes a day ahead. When ready to cook or bake, add the wine, broth (or water), drizzle with oil and sprinkle with more cheese.

EGGPLANT PARMIGIANA

serves: 6-8 ·········· time: 2hrs ··········

This fried casserole has a crispy baked exterior with a soft and salty center. Every last morsel is graced with the incomparable flavour combination of tomato sauce, and melted cheese caressing the salted and fried flavour sponge.

EQUIPMENT
Baking Dish

INGREDIENTS
4 cups tomato sauce

2 kg (3 - 4) firm eggplants

3 - 4 Tbsp salt (for sweating)

1 ½ cups all purpose flour

salt and ground pepper, to taste

½ tsp dried oregano

2 cups (approx.) vegetable oil for frying

1 cup freshly grated parmesan

500 g mozzarella, shredded

2 Tbsp torn fresh basil

DIRECTIONS
Refer to page 198 in the BASICS chapter for Tomato Sauce recipe.

Have the tomato sauce made or cook it while the eggplant "sweats".

Slice eggplants into 1 cm thick rounds or long slices. Leave unpeeled (except for the outer slices). Sprinkle both sides with salt, layer the slices on a rack, over a baking pan; cover the slices with a layer of paper towels, weigh down with something heavy like a cutting board, to draw out moisture, and let "sweat" for at least 30 minutes. After moisture has released, gently squeeze and pat-dry with paper towels.

Combine flour, salt, pepper and dried oregano in a shallow pan. Lightly dredge eggplant slices in flour mixture before frying.

In a large pan, heat enough oil, over high heat, to generously coat the bottom of the pan. When hot, add eggplant slices, without overlapping, and fry until golden brown, about 2 minutes, on each side; transfer to a rack lined with paper towels, to drain.

Repeat until all the eggplant slices are fried; add more oil as needed but heat it first, so that the eggplant sizzles, on first touch.

Preheat oven to 375°F (190°C).

To assemble, have the tomato sauce, fried eggplant, grated parmesan, shredded mozzarella and basil ready.

Spread a thin layer of tomato sauce in a large baking dish (22 x 30 cm). Add a layer of eggplant slices, overlapping slightly, if necessary. Cover with sauce, top with shredded mozzarella, sprinkle with parmesan and some fresh torn basil leaves. Repeat

MELANZANE ALLA PARMIGIANA

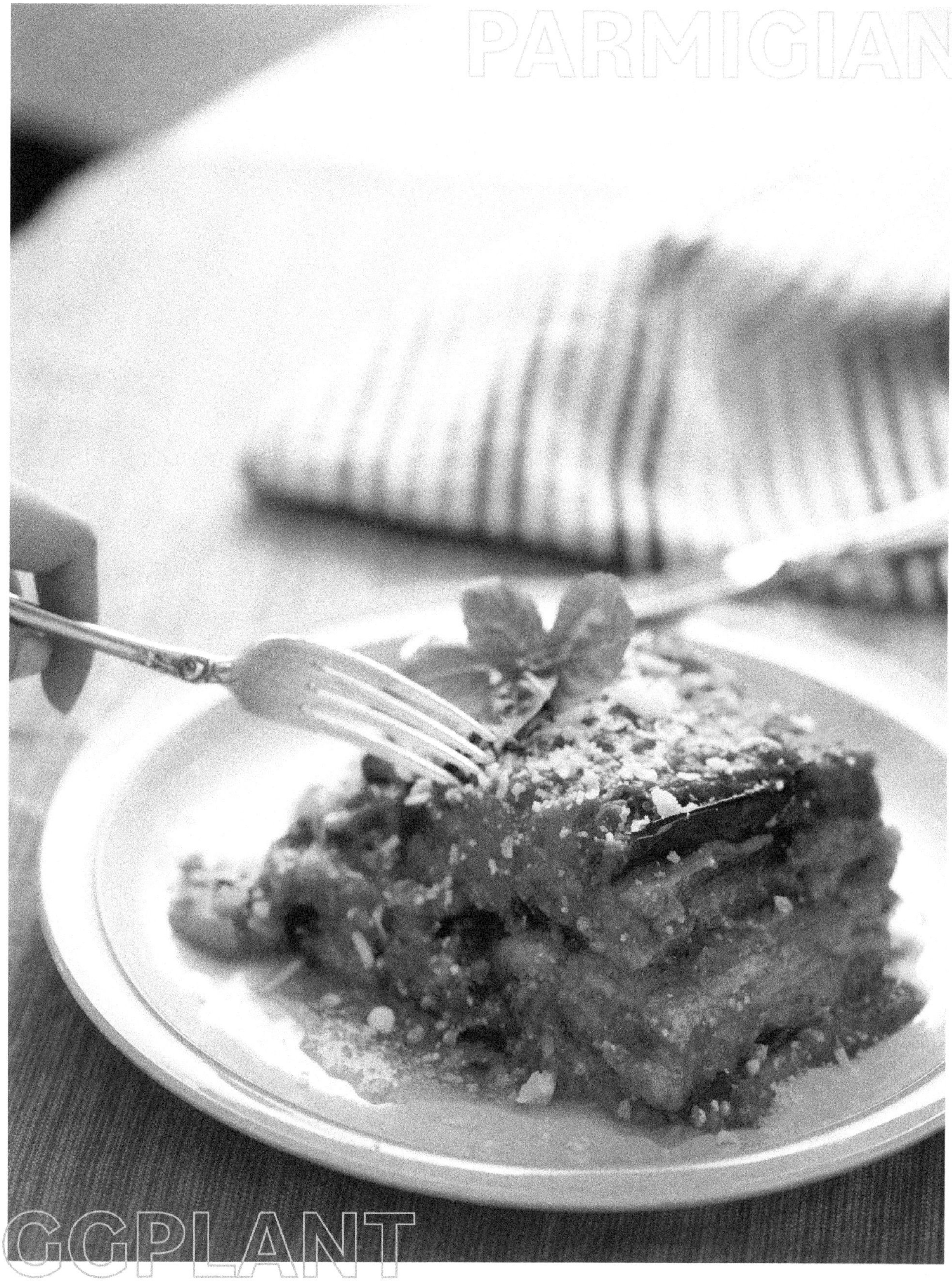

EGGPLANT
EGGPLANT

with two or more layers. Top the final layer with more sauce and a generous sprinkle of parmesan.

Cover in foil and bake at 375°F (190°C) for 35 minutes.

Remove foil and bake for another 10 minutes, or place under broiler for a few minutes, until cheese starts to brown.

Let rest 10 minutes. Serve, either hot, warm or cold.

STEF SAYS

Give it some crunch! After sweating and patting the eggplant dry, give it the full crumbing treatment. Transfer eggplant slices from flour, to an egg wash then into bread crumbs for final coating, all before frying.

PEPERONATA

serves: 4-6 .... time: 1hr 30mins ....

Deliciously sweet, colourful and very versatile, these stewed bell peppers can be enjoyed as a tasty side dish for meats, as an appetizer with crusty bread, or as a sauce over pasta or polenta.

INGREDIENTS

½ cup olive oil

4 garlic cloves, crushed

1 large white onion, thinly sliced

4 multi-coloured bell peppers, washed, seeded and thinly sliced (1.5 cm)

½ cup white wine

1 cup passata or peeled whole plum tomatoes, roughly chopped

½ tsp hot chilli pepper flakes or fresh peperoncino, finely chopped

salt and ground pepper

2 Tbsp of fresh basil, torn or chopped

DIRECTIONS

In a large pan, heat the oil over medium heat; add the garlic and let sizzle, but not burn, until fragrant, 1 minute. Add the onions; stir and sauté until combined, 1 - 2 minutes.

Add the peppers, stir and coat well with oil and cook until the peppers start to soften, about 15 minutes.

Raise to high heat, add wine and cook until lightly reduced, about 1 – 2 minutes.

Add the tomatoes and season with chilli flakes, salt and pepper.

Reduce heat to low, cover and simmer peppers, stirring occasionally, for another 25 - 30 minutes – the key is slow cooking! When ready, the peppers will be soft and translucent in a syrup-like glaze.

If the peppers become too dry, during the cooking process, splash some water or wine, to keep them moist.

Adjust seasoning and sprinkle with fresh basil. Serve hot or cold.

MAMMA'S TIPS

Poach some eggs in it! Move the peppers to create wells, crack an egg in each well, season with salt and pepper, cover and poach the last 6 – 8 minutes of simmering.

STEF SAYS

Put Peperonata to top your Italian Sausage-on-a-Bun.

CHEF'S NOTES

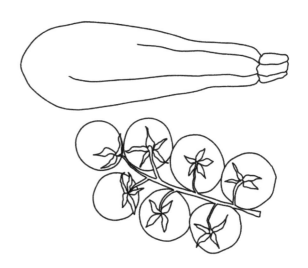

Chapter 4
PASTA

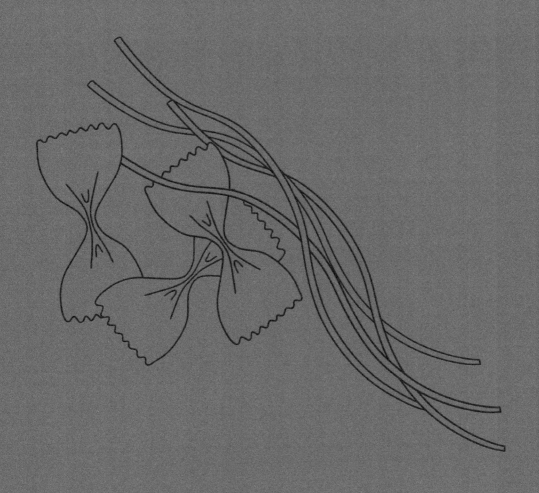

SPAGHETTI ALLA CARBONARA

serves: 4-5 .... time: 30mins ....

Spaghetti alla Carbonara glorifies the concept of breakfast for dinner, with the thought of bacon, eggs, and parmesan. But it's not bacon, nor pancetta that is the preferred cut of pork in this Roman dish, instead, it's the jowl cut, known as guanciale. It's also meant to be pecorino cheese rather than parmesan, so some pre-conceptions may be shattered! We've perfected the dish with the original ingredients, but the skies won't fall if you substitute to make your carbonara dreams come true. Guanciale > pancetta > bacon / pecorino > parmesan - prioritize from left to right or combine. Either way, it's going to be good!

INGREDIENTS

450 g guanciale cut into 5 cm (2-inch) cubes or slices

500 g spaghetti or other pasta

2 eggs

½ cup (60 g) grated pecorino or parmesan

sea salt and freshly cracked pepper

pasta water (up to 2 cups)

DIRECTIONS

Heat a large pan to high heat; add the guanciale and cook until brown and crispy, about 6 - 8 minutes.

With a slotted spoon, transfer the guanciale aside, leave the grease in the pan; remove the pan from heat and set aside to cool down.

Bring a large pot of salted water to a boil. Add the pasta to the boiling water and cook a minute shy of al dente. Midway through cooking, scoop out 1 cup of the starchy pasta water and reserve.

In a medium bowl, whisk the eggs with the pecorino and season with salt and pepper. Whisk the egg mixture with one hand and slowly drizzle the pasta water into the eggs with the other hand. Keep whisking to incorporate the water without scrambling the eggs.

When the pasta is nearly al dente, reserve another cup of pasta water.

Use tongs to transfer the pasta into the pan with the cooled guanciale grease. Gradually mix the pasta with one hand, drizzle the egg mixture slowly with the other hand, making sure the eggs don't cook to a scramble. Continue to toss vigorously while adding small amounts of the reserved pasta water.

Toss until the mixture forms a glossy sauce and coats all of the pasta; add more pasta water if the coating is not glossy.

Add half of the guanciale pieces and toss to combine.

Serve immediately, garnished with the reserved guanciale, pepper and extra grated pecorino.

STEF SAYS

Separate an egg and place the yolk on top of each serving for a richer and more golden coating.

Don't put cream in carbonara!

PENNE ALLA VODKA

serves: 4-5 .... time: 25mins ....

This boozed up rosée is a simple satisfier. Rich and glossy, the vodka enhances the tomato fruitiness and sweetens the perfect catalyst in this shimmering tomato-cream marriage.

INGREDIENTS

Refer to page 198 in the BASICS chapter for Tomato Sauce ingredients and directions.

100 g pancetta, very finely diced

1 cup vodka

2 cups tomato sauce

¼ tsp cayenne or chilli pepper, or to suit taste

salt and pepper, to taste

1 cup heavy cream

2 Tbsp butter

500 g penne rigate or other short pasta

8 fresh basil leaves, torn or chopped, for garnish

freshly grated parmesan

DIRECTIONS

Have prepared tomato sauce ready.

Bring a large pot of salted water to a boil. Add penne and cook, al dente, according to package directions. Reserve 1 cup of pasta water before draining pasta.

In a deep pan, cook pancetta, on medium-high, for about 5 minutes or until crispy.

Add vodka and bring to a boiling point; cook and reduce by half (a few minutes).

Add the tomato sauce, bring to a boil, reduce heat to low and simmer for about 5 minutes; season, to taste, with cayenne or chilli pepper, salt and pepper.

Stir in cream and heat until sauce returns to a gentle roll; add the butter and turn heat to the lowest possible simmer or remove from heat, until pasta is cooked.

With the sauce pan on low heat, transfer drained pasta into the sauce; toss and coat well. If sauce is too thick, thin with half a cup or more of pasta water and continue tossing until smooth and glossy.

Garnish with fresh chopped basil and serve with freshly grated parmesan.

MAMMA'S TIPS

For a richer sauce, substitute the Basic Tomato Sauce for the Smooth Meat Sauce as found on page 202 in the Basics section.

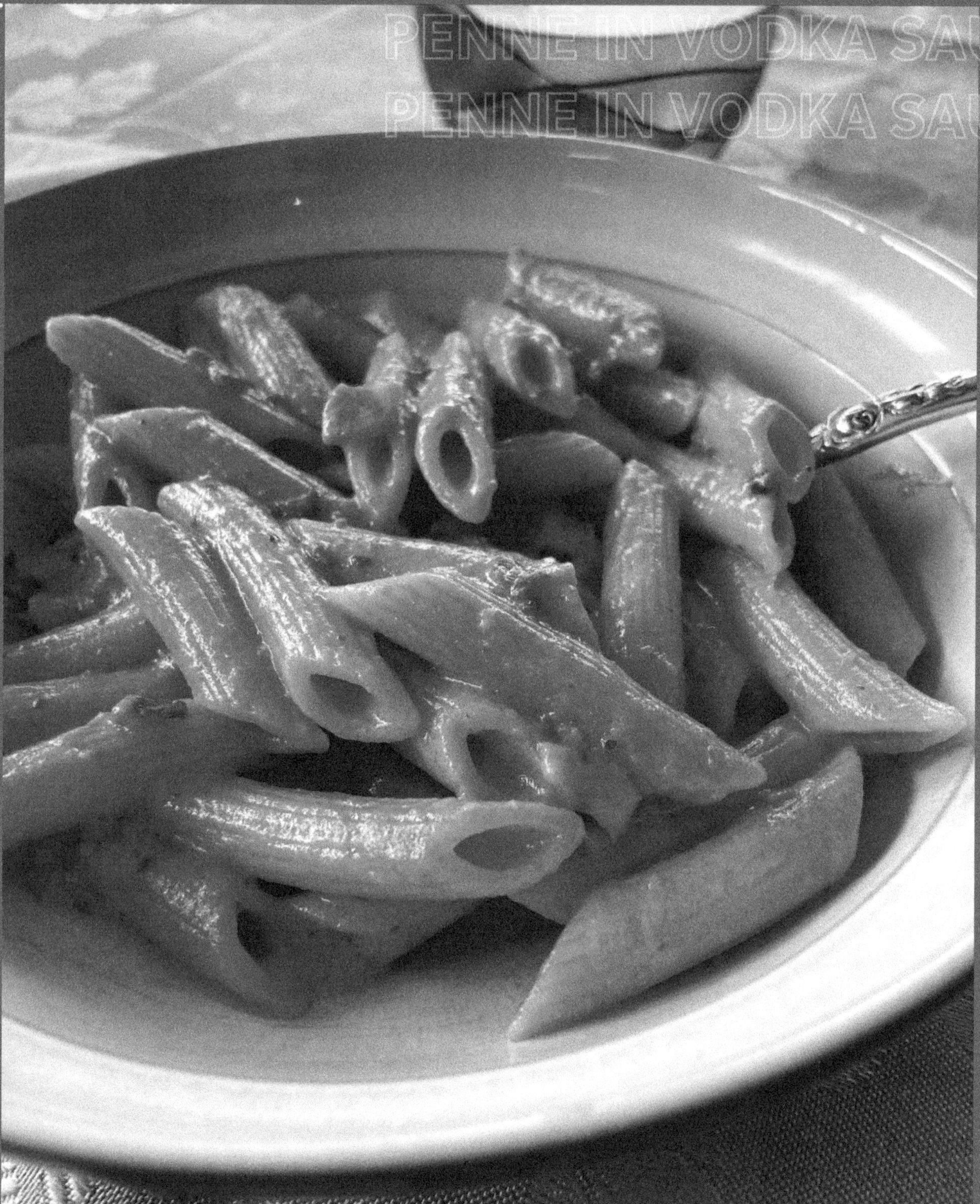

LINGUINE ALLE VONGOLE

serves: 4-5 .... time: 40mins ....

This elegant pasta dish, in a garlicky white wine sauce, is not only impressive and delicious, it is also quick and simple to make. Perfect on a hot day with a cold glass of dry white wine.

INGREDIENTS

300 g canned/jarred baby clams, drained and liquid reserved

2 cups liquid (white wine + reserved clam liquid)

6 Tbsp olive oil

4 garlic cloves, crushed

salt and pepper, to taste

¼ tsp dried chilli pepper flakes, or to taste

½ tsp turmeric (optional)

500 g linguine pasta

3 Tbsp butter

2 Tbsp finely chopped fresh parsley

freshly ground pepper

DIRECTIONS

Place a small colander in a bowl; drain jarred clams and keep the liquid. Rinse clams and cleanse with a splash of white wine; set aside.

Strain the clam liquid through a sieve and pour into a 2-cup container. Add white wine to fill the container; set aside.

In a large pot, bring salted water to a boil, for the pasta.

Meanwhile, in a large pan, on medium-high, heat oil and garlic; stir and cook for about 30 seconds, until fragrant but not browned. Add the wine and clam liquid; bring to a boil and cook briskly, until foam disappears and liquid is reduced by about half. Season liquid with salt, pepper, chilli pepper flakes and turmeric.

Add drained clams to the sauce. Stir, bring back to a boil and remove from heat. Add butter and 1 Tbsp of the chopped parsley. Drain cooked linguine; toss with sauce and drained linguine over low heat; garnish with more fresh parsley and ground pepper; serve at once.

MAMMA'S TIPS

For added colour and taste, add some halved cherry tomatoes to the sauce.

STEF SAYS

Use 1 Kg of fresh clams; scrub well in cold water, remove any that are opened. Steam in a covered pot with 1 cup of white wine until they open (3 - 5 minutes), (discard any that don't); remove from heat and liquid. Set aside until final stage.

SPAGHETTI ALLA PUTTANESCA

serves: 4-5 .... time: 30mins ....

Pasta, "the way a whore would make it," originated in Naples... really, that's the etymology! The prostitutes would serve a plate of pasta to their customers to keep them happy while waiting their turn. Between clients, the ladies would prepare this quick, cheap and easy to make meal, using ingredients that were readily available. The piquant aroma of this deliciously hot and frisky dish would attract and entice, yearning clients off the street.

INGREDIENTS

800 ml canned plum tomatoes, roughly crushed

6 Tbsp olive oil

4 garlic cloves, finely chopped

finely chopped fresh chilli pepper or dried flakes, to taste

4 anchovy fillets, roughly chopped

¼ cup capers, drained and rinsed

1 cup whole, pitted, drained, black olives

salt and pepper, to taste

2 Tbsp fresh parsley, finely chopped

500 g spaghetti

1 cup reserved pasta water

freshly grated parmesan

DIRECTIONS

Pour the canned tomatoes in a bowl and crush to your preferred texture, with your hands or a wooden spoon.

Heat oil in a large saucepan, on medium-high heat. Add garlic, chilli peppers and anchovies. Cook to release the fragrance, 30 seconds; add the capers and olives, stir to combine and cook for another minute. Add the tomatoes; season with salt and pepper, being careful not to oversalt as the olives and capers are already salty. Bring to a boil, reduce heat to medium and simmer for 10 - 15 minutes.

In the meantime, bring a large pot of salted water to a boil, for the pasta. When water boils, add the spaghetti.

Before spaghetti reaches the al dente stage, set aside 1 cup of pasta water; drain and toss spaghetti into the sauce, allowing it to finish cooking there. Add the parsley, and if necessary, some of the reserved pasta water, to allow the sauce to coat and gloss over the spaghetti.

Serve with freshly grated parmesan cheese.

SPAGHETTI
PUTTANESCA

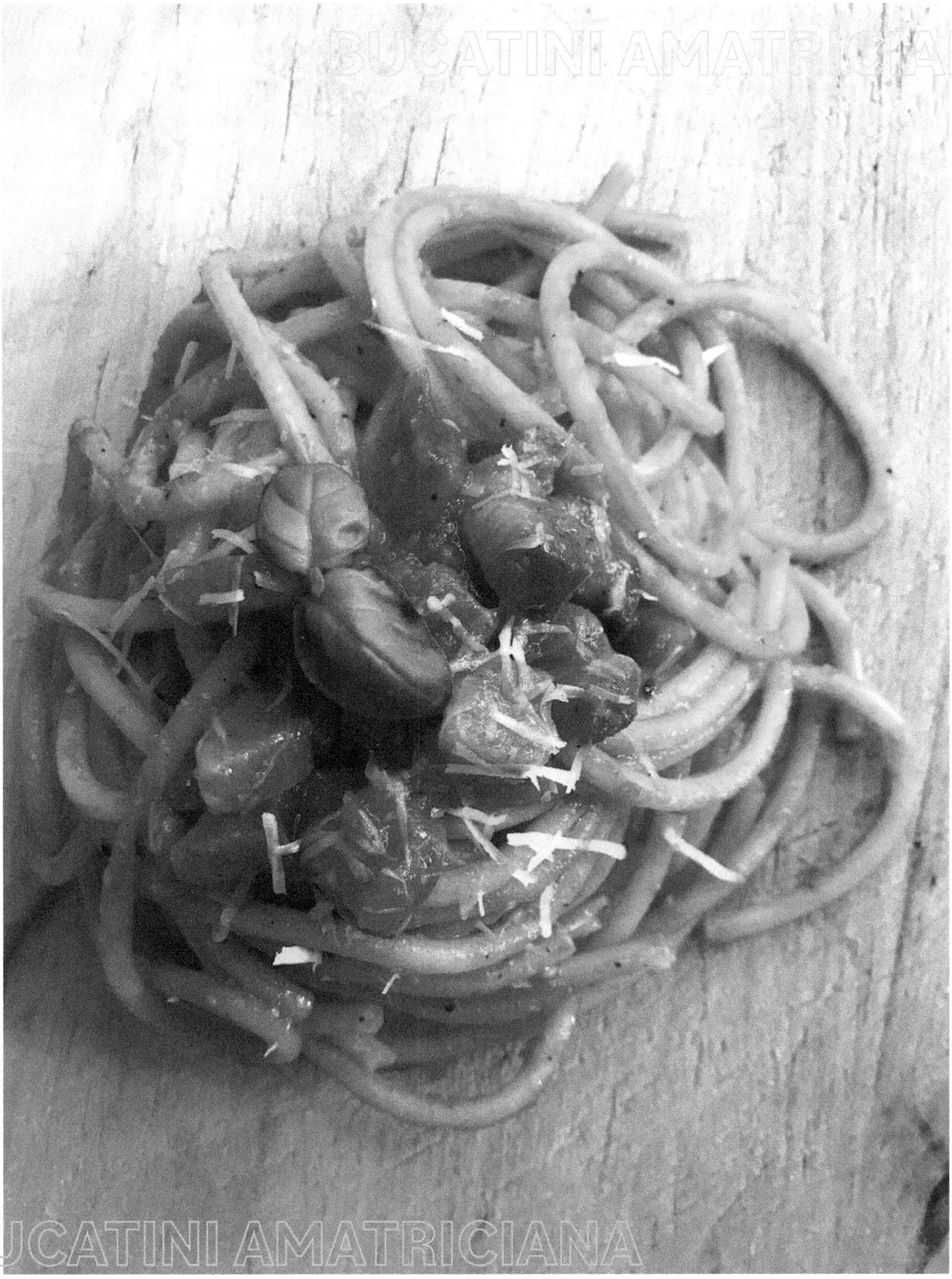

BUCATINI ALL' AMATRICIANA

serves: 4-5 .... time: 35mins ....

Simply put, it's tomato, cheese and pork. Similar to the carbonara, the pork-cut "should be" guanciale, but if pancetta or bacon avail themselves, they'll do a wonderful job too. The cheese "should be" pecorino, but in a pinch parmesan will do the job. Keep it authentic or make it your own. As in the carbonara, it's another Roman sauce that doesn't require oil or butter because of the generous lubricating emission the guanciale provides.

INGREDIENTS

200 g guanciale (5 mm thick slices and cubed)

1 small sweet onion, finely chopped

½ - 1 tsp chilli flakes (peperoncino)

3 cups (800 ml can) Italian plum tomatoes

salt and pepper, to taste

4 sprigs fresh basil

500 g bucatini pasta

1 cup reserved pasta water

¾ cup grated pecorino

DIRECTIONS

In a large pan, heat guanciale (or pancetta). Cook over medium-high heat, until guanciale is crisp and transparent, and has emitted a liquified fat, about 5 minutes. Add onion and chilli pepper flakes; reduce to medium heat and sauté until onions are softened, another 5 minutes or so.

Pour the canned plum tomatoes in a bowl and roughly crush and break down, to your preferred texture, with your hands or a wooden spoon, then add to the pan.

Season with salt and pepper. Cook for about 15 minutes, stirring frequently.

Add basil and adjust seasoning, to taste.

Bring salted water to a boil; add bucatini and cook to al dente. Set aside 1 cup of pasta water; drain and toss bucatini into the sauce. If sauce is too thick, thin with some of the reserved pasta water, to allow the sauce to coat and gloss over the pasta. Toss and serve with grated pecorino.

MAMMA'S TIPS

This sauce is delicious with gnocchi too.

PASTA CON SUGO DI TONNO

serves: 4-6 .... time: 30mins ....

A long-standing Christmas Eve tradition in our family, this nautical twist to a tomato-based sauce has since become a healthy and favourite year-round option. As always, most any pasta will do, but in our family, the choice is very much a point of debate! Will it be the traditional Zitoni, messy but fun to eat since they ingest so much sauce then squirt it back at you when you twirl your fork (and where a bib and a knife are highly recommended), or will it be the Mezzi Rigatoni, tasty, neat and according to Mamma, very civilized? Whatever the choice, you will love this sauce on any pasta!

INGREDIENTS

2 Tbsp olive oil

2 - 3 garlic cloves, crushed

2 anchovy fillets, finely chopped

½ tsp hot pepper, minced, or dried chilli flakes, to taste

½ cup white wine

800 ml crushed tomatoes (passata)

½ cup water, to rinse container and add to tomatoes

salt and pepper, to taste

3 - 160 g (5 oz) canned or jarred tuna in olive oil, undrained

3 Tbsp capers, drained

1 cup pitted whole green olives, halved or quartered

2 Tbsp freshly chopped parsley

500 g zitoni, mezzi rigatoni or pasta of choice

DIRECTIONS

Heat oil with garlic, anchovies and chilli flakes and sauté until fragrant, about 1 minute. Add wine and cook on high heat, until mostly evaporated,1 - 2 minutes. Add tomatoes and water; season with salt and pepper. Bring to a boil, reduce heat to medium-low and simmer for about 15 - 20 minutes, stirring occasionally until sauce has reached a desirable consistency.

Add the tuna (with the oil), capers, olives and half the parsley and continue simmering for another 10 minutes.

In the meantime, bring a large pot of salted water to a boil and cook pasta, al dente, according to package instructions.

Reserve a cup of pasta water, then drain. Toss the zitoni well with the sauce. If necessary, add some pasta water to keep the sauce fluid and the pasta glossy. Garnish with remaining chopped parsley.

Serve – without grated cheese!

PASTA IN TUNA SAUCE
PASTA IN TUNA SAUCE
PASTA IN TUNA SAUCE

TUNA
TUNA

STROZZAPRETI ALLA NORMA

serves: 4-6 .... time: 1hr 30mins ....

"This is the real Norma!" exclaimed a Sicilian writer, upon being served this new dish, in honour of Bellini's opera, "Norma", premiering that same night. A perfect blend of eggplant, tomato sauce and freshly grated ricotta salata, paired here with strozzapreti or "priest chokers"... an elongated hand-rolled, twisty, and often "egg-less" pasta type.

INGREDIENTS

800 g (about 2) firm eggplants

1 Tbsp salt, to sweat eggplant

½ cup + 4 Tbsp olive oil

800 ml canned plum tomatoes, or 10 - 12 fresh plum tomatoes, blanched, skinned, squeezed and coarsely chopped or pulsed

½ cup water, to rinse can and add to tomatoes

2 cloves garlic, crushed

1 small onion, finely chopped

½ cup white wine

salt & freshly ground pepper, to taste

½ tsp red pepper flakes

500 g strozzapreti pasta

1 cup reserved pasta water

8 - 10 fresh basil leaves, torn

150 g (approx.) freshly grated ricotta salata, for serving

DIRECTIONS

Cut eggplant into thick, 2 cm slices, then cut slices into 2 cm cubes.

Place in a colander, over a bowl, sprinkle with salt, toss, weigh down with a plate, to draw out moisture and let "sweat" for 30 minutes. (If using the preferred round Sicilian eggplants, sweating is optional as they are more fleshy, less watery and not as bitter).

Gently squeeze and dry with a clean cloth or paper towels.

In a large frying pan, heat ¼ cup of olive oil; when very hot, but not smoking, add eggplant cubes. Fry in batches, adding more oil for each batch. Turn and fry the cubes, on all sides, over high heat, until golden; drain on paper towels and set aside.

MAMMA'S TIPS

Instead of frying, drizzle the eggplant cubes in olive oil, season with salt and pepper, spread out on a baking sheet and roast in a hot 450°F (240°C) oven for about 25 minutes.

FOR THE SAUCE

Pour tomatoes in a bowl; crush and break down roughly, with your hands or wooden spoon; wash down tomato can with ½ cup of water and add to bowl; set aside until needed (or prepare the fresh tomatoes).

Heat 4 Tbsp of olive oil in a large deep pan, over medium heat. Add garlic and onion; sauté for 5 - 6 minutes, until onions are soft and translucent. Raise heat to med-high and add wine; cook until mostly evaporated, 1 - 2 minutes.

Add tomatoes; season with salt, pepper and chilli flakes. Bring to a boil and reduce heat to medium; simmer and cook, partly covered, for 15 - 20 minutes or until sauce has thickened.

Add the eggplant cubes; gently stir to blend the flavours. Remove from heat or simmer on lowest heat setting, until pasta is ready.

Cook pasta, in boiling salted water, 'al dente', according to directions. Reserve one cup of pasta water before draining pasta. Toss pasta in the simmering sauce; add some pasta water, if needed, to keep the sauce fluid and pasta well-coated and glossy .

Plate, sprinkle with fresh basil leaves and grated ricotta salata.

STEF SAYS

Add a pinch of cinnamon when you add the eggplant to the sauce, stir and blend flavours and enjoy a sweet aromatic touch to your Norma.

FUSILLI CON PESTO GENOVESE

serves: 4 .... time: 40mins ....

Traditionally made with mortar and pestle, this popular fresh basil summer sauce can be easily prepared in a food processor, in minutes. Enjoy freshly made, tossed over cooked fusilli pasta or seal tightly in small containers and freeze.

EQUIPMENT

Food Processor

INGREDIENTS

2 packed cups (approx 125 g) fresh basil leaves (stems removed, washed, drained)

½ cup olive oil

2 large cloves garlic

¼ cup pine nuts, toasted + extra for garnish

½ tsp salt

500 g fusilli pasta

4 Tbsp soft butter

¾ - 1 cup reserved pasta water

2 Tbsp freshly grated parmesan or romano (pecorino) cheese + more for serving

salt and fresh ground pepper, to taste

DIRECTIONS

In a small frying pan, on stove-top, toast the pine nuts, in a single layer, over medium heat. Toss gently until golden, 3 - 5 minutes.

Wash, drain and spread out basil leaves on a tray; pat dry with clean cloth or paper towels to remove excess water.

In a food processor, combine basil, oil, garlic, pine nuts, and salt. Process for about 10 seconds, scrape sides of bowl with a spatula, continue to process a few more seconds, until mixture is smooth and well blended (if freezing, freeze at this stage). Transfer to a small mixing bowl.

Cook pasta in boiling salted water to al dente. Before pasta is cooked, reserve 1 cup of pasta water. Add ½ cup of pasta water, 2 Tbsp butter and 2 Tbsp of grated cheese to the pesto in the bowl; stir to a thin saucy consistency.

Drain pasta and return to the pot, on stove, at low heat. Toss pasta with the pesto sauce, the remaining butter and, if needed, more of the pasta water, so that a smooth, glossy sauce is achieved. Serve with freshly ground pepper and grated cheese; garnish with extra toasted pine nuts or fresh basil leaves.

SPAGHETTI AGLIO, OLIO E PEPERONCINO

serves: 4-5 .... time: 20mins ....

This Roman staple is a pick-me-up dish. It is flavourful, delicious, and super simple to make. For many Italians, it is the go-to snack after an evening out with friends. Whether 11:00 pm or 3:00 am, it's a natural late night necessity to gather at someone's home for a spuntino (snack) of aglio, olio e peperoncino.

INGREDIENTS

500 g spaghetti

½ cup extra virgin olive oil

4 - 6 garlic cloves, minced or thinly sliced

1 tsp (or to taste) crushed chilli pepper flakes or peperoncino, fresh hot pepper, seeded and finely chopped

salt and freshly ground pepper, to taste

½ cup reserved pasta water

2 Tbsp finely chopped parsley

good quality olive oil, for drizzling

freshly grated parmesan

DIRECTIONS

Set a large pot of salted water to boil. Cook the spaghetti according to package instructions, until just shy of al dente.

While the pasta is cooking, combine the olive oil, garlic, chilli flakes, salt and pepper in a large pan. Cook slowly over medium-low heat, for about 5 minutes, letting the oil absorb the flavours of the garlic and chilli flakes without letting anything burn. Remove from heat before garlic browns.

When the pasta is almost al dente, reserve the pasta water, then, drain and transfer pasta to the seasoned oil in the pan, along with ½ cup of the pasta water. Turn the heat up to medium-high. Stir and toss until the sauce has emulsified and coats the pasta.

Garnish with chopped parsley, toss and serve with a drizzle of good quality olive oil and grated parmesan over top.

MAMMA'S TIPS

For a more flavourful salty punch, chop one or two anchovy fillets and add to the heating oil.

CHEF'S NOTES

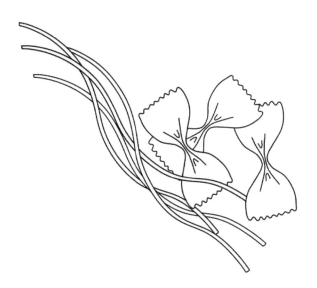

Chapter 5

STUFFED AND BAKED PASTA

ARTICHOKE AGNOLOTTI IN ROSÉ SAUCE

yields: 24-26 ·········· time: 2hrs ·········· Advanced ··········

Pasta formed and stuffed to resemble a pillow makes it a more legitimate comfort food... right? This recipe refers you back to our foolproof pasta dough, to shape and stuff, with a sweet artichoke filling, before smothering in a creamy rosé sauce.

EQUIPMENT

Food Processor

Pasta Machine

Pasta Cutters

STEP 1 INGREDIENTS

1 cup whole-milk ricotta, drained

zest and juice of ½ lemon + a bowl of water

10 small fresh artichokes, with stems, cleaned/quartered

4 Tbsp olive oil

1 shallot, chopped

1 garlic clove, chopped

salt and pepper, to taste

1 Tbsp fresh thyme or parsley, chopped

¼ tsp chilli pepper flakes

½ cup white wine

1 cup broth or water

1 egg + 1 egg yolk, lightly beaten (reserve white for egg wash)

¼ tsp grated nutmeg, or to taste

¾ cup grated parmesan

STEP 1 – FILLING

DIRECTIONS

Wrap the ricotta in a cheesecloth and set in a sieve to drain. Refrigerate until needed.

Zest half a lemon and set aside. Squeeze the juice from the lemon half in a medium bowl of cold water.

Clean and trim artichokes. Cut off top third and discard; tear off dark outer leaves, leaving only the light, tender inner leaves.

Cut artichokes in quarters, remove the fuzzy center, the choke, and place cleaned and cut artichokes in the lemon water, to prevent discolouring.

The stems are very meaty and sweet; peel off and discard their outer skin and add stems to lemon water. Drain well and pat dry before using.

In a heavy pan, on medium heat, heat oil and sauté onion and garlic, until softened and fragrant, 3 - 5 minutes. Add artichokes, stir and cook until well-coated, about 5 minutes. Season with salt and pepper, thyme or parsley and chilli flakes. Raise heat, add wine and cook until almost evaporated. Add broth or water, cover and cook over medium heat, for about 30 - 40 minutes, stirring often, until artichokes are very tender, and all the liquid has evaporated.

Add more liquid, if mixture dries up before the artichokes are soft, tender and cooked. Season to taste. Remove from heat and cool slightly.

97

STEP 4 INGREDIENTS

2 Tbsp olive oil

2 Tbsp butter

2 garlic cloves, crushed

1 shallot finely chopped

2 cups tomato passata

½ tsp sugar

¼ tsp hot chili flakes, or to taste

4 - 6 basil leaves, finely chopped,
or 1 tsp dried

salt and pepper, to taste

2 Tbsp goat cheese (optional)

1 cup cream

freshly grated pecorino or
parmesan

Transfer artichoke mixture to a food processing bowl and pulse to a paste.

Place mixture in a bowl; add the ricotta, beaten eggs, lemon zest, nutmeg and parmesan cheese. Season to taste, mix well to combine and refrigerate until ready to fill the agnolotti.

STEP 2 - PASTA DOUGH

DIRECTIONS
Refer to page 193 in the BASICS chapter for Pasta Dough recipe for 6 - 8 servings.

STEP 3 - ASSEMBLY

DIRECTIONS
For filled pasta, stretch the dough on the pasta machine to about #5 or one number thicker than the traditional pasta recipe so that it can hold the filling and not fall apart.

Place two stretched pasta strips, side by side. Place spoonfuls of filling, in a line, along the centre of one strip, about 5 cm apart; brush around the fillings with egg-wash; place the other strip directly on top. Cup and press around each filling, to eliminate excess air and to seal properly, then, use a round cutter to shape your agnolotti. Crimp or press around edges securely. Re-use the cut-out dough if it is clean and fresh.

Place on a sheet pan with flour or cornmeal, to prevent bottoms from sticking and to dry, while completing the others.

Use right away or lay flat on a parchment-lined tray and freeze. When frozen, transfer to a sealed freezer bag.

STEP 4 - SAUCE

DIRECTIONS
Heat oil and butter in a saucepan, over medium heat. Add the shallots and garlic and sauté until softened and fragrant, about 3 - 5 minutes.

Add tomato passata, sugar, chilli flakes, basil, salt and pepper. Simmer, covered, about 5 - 10 minutes. Add the goat cheese and cream.

Bring back to a bubble and remove from heat.

COOK THE AGNOLOTTI
Bring a large pot of salted water to a boil.

STEF SAYS

Crumble a pinch of goat cheese over
the top of each serving for
a tart and earthy kick.

Set aside, and add at the final stage.

Add the agnolotti; return water to a boil and cook until agnolotti float to the surface. Remove the agnolotti, with a slotted spoon and transfer to the saucepan. Toss gently and, if needed, add enough pasta water to make the sauce fluid and glossy.

Transfer to plate and serve with grated pecorino or parmesan.

MAMMA'S TIPS

Reduce time: replace fresh with 400 g of canned artichoke hearts, (drained, squeeze-dried of all moisture and cut into quarters). Sauté in oil with shallots and garlic; season; cook down with wine until evaporated; remove from heat; cool; transfer to food processor and continue with recipe directions.

MAC & CHEESE WITH SQUASH

serves: 4-6 .... time: 1hr 30mins ....

To the lip-smacking delight of her children and without any notice, Mamma improvised a way to slip some veg into her kids' sought-after food. The squash, in this traditional "American" dish, compliments the colour, thickens the sauce and makes for a lighter, healthier and even tastier option than you'd expect.

EQUIPMENT

Hand Blender

Food Processor

Baking Dish

INGREDIENTS

1 medium (500 g) squash (butternut, hubbard), peeled, seeds removed and cubed

1½ cups chicken broth

2 garlic cloves

1 Tbsp butter

½ tsp each of salt and pepper, or to taste

½ tsp each nutmeg, cayenne and dry mustard

3 cups (300 g) combined shredded cheeses - cheddar, gruyere or swiss

2 cups light cream or milk

½ cup grated parmesan

500 g macaroni (shells, large ditali, elbow…)

1 cup reserved pasta water

TOPPING

1 Tbsp butter

1 cup panko crumbs

2 Tbsp grated parmesan

DIRECTIONS

Butter a deep baking dish and set aside.

Measure and set aside shredded cheese and required ingredients.

Combine the peeled and cubed squash, broth and garlic in a medium saucepan; bring to a boil, and cook, covered, over medium heat, until squash is tender (about 25 minutes).

While squash cooks:
a) Prepare panko crumb topping: Heat butter in a small pan; add panko crumbs and cook for 2 - 3 minutes, until they begin to turn golden. Remove from heat, stir in the grated parmesan and set aside.

b) Bring a pot of salted water to a boil and cook pasta to al dente. When cooked, reserve one cup of pasta water, then drain the pasta and immediately rinse in cold water to prevent further cooking; place in a large bowl and set aside.

c) Preheat oven to 375°F (190°C)

When squash is cooked, add butter and remove pot from the heat. Using a hand-blender, purée squash with its liquid, directly in the pot (or transfer to a food processor and purée).

Place the puréed squash in a large bowl and season with salt, pepper, nutmeg, cayenne and dry mustard. Stir in the shredded cheeses and combine. Add the cream or milk and grated parmesan. Mix well and season, to taste.

Add the squash and cheese mixture to the pasta; toss until evenly combined, and if required, thin down with some of the reserved pasta water. The mixture should be of a thin consistency and spread very easily, as the pasta will absorb a lot of liquid during baking.

Pour the mixture into the buttered baking dish and sprinkle the panko topping evenly over the pasta.

Bake uncovered for 25 - 30 minutes or until bubbly. Broil for 1 - 2 minutes for a more desired browning. Serve immediately.

MAMMA'S TIPS

May be prepared, covered and refrigerated a day ahead, before baking (or frozen, then thawed and baked when needed).

STEF SAYS

Add crispy bacon bits on top of individual servings.

LASAGNA

serves: 10-12 .... time: 5hrs .... Advanced ....

In Le Marche, this dish was often referred to as vincisgrassi or timballo (with the layers of goodness enclosed or wrapped entirely within sheets of fresh pasta, like a gift). Today it is better known as lasagna, a delicate baked dish of layered fresh pasta sheets filled with a rich blend of meat sauce and cheeses. Making lasagna from scratch requires many stages of preparation, all of which are well worth the effort. Mamma's recipe is a perfect balance of new and traditional and – without a shadow of a doubt – the tastiest.

EQUIPMENT

Pasta Machine

Deep Baking Dish, approx.

28 x 23 x 6cm

INGREDIENTS

prepared bolognese sauce

5 cups (500 g) (approx.) shredded or sliced bocconcini

4 cups (400 g) (approx.) shredded mozzarella

1½ cups (150 g) freshly grated parmesan

½ cup butter, cut in small cubes

prepared lasagna (pasta) strips

STEP 1 – BOLOGNESE SAUCE

DIRECTIONS

Refer to page 201 in the BASICS chapter for Bolognese sauce recipe. Sauce may be made a day ahead and refrigerated.

STEP 2 – PASTA DOUGH

DIRECTIONS

Refer to page 193 in the BASICS chapter for Pasta Dough recipe. Prepare based on proportions for 10 - 12. Make, cover and let rest for at least 30 minutes.

STEP 3 – MAKE LASAGNA STRIPS

Set the pasta machine on the first setting. On a floured wooden board, cut a piece of dough, about the size of an English muffin (always keep unused dough well covered). Flatten, lightly flour and run the dough through the first or widest setting on the pasta machine. If not smooth or even, fold and run through the first setting a few more times.

Proceed with the second setting and continue with subsequent numbers, on the machine, keeping the dough smooth and lightly floured. Make dough as thin as possible, without tearing it (transparent enough to see your fingers through it). The second to last number (#7) is usually a good final setting, but it varies with each machine.

If the dough strip gets too long, cut in half and proceed with the process.

Place each strip of dough on a lightly floured tablecloth (or drying rack) until all are done. Lay smoothly without overlapping.

STEP 4 – LASAGNA ASSEMBLY

DIRECTIONS

Generously butter a deep baking dish for the lasagna. Set up an assembly area with the pot of sauce and ladle, a bowl with the bocconcini, a bowl with the mozzarella, a bowl with the grated parmesan and a bowl with butter cubes.

Place a cutting board covered with a clean tea towel next to the buttered lasagna pan. Have some clean kitchen towels nearby.

Bring a large pot of salted water to a boil. Have another deep wide pan ready with cold water and a few drops of oil in it. Have slotted or wooden spoons and/or strainer nearby.

When water boils, carefully add 2 - 3 strips of dough (begin with longer ones). Stir gently with a wooden spoon until the water returns to a gentle boil; reduce heat and carefully, with the wooden and slotted spoon, transfer strips into the cold water bath. (Reduce or turn off heat and proceed to assemble a few layers of the lasagna, before boiling more dough strips).

Spread a thin layer of sauce in the buttered pan.

Take one cooked lasagna strip at a time and place on the tea towel to absorb the excess water.

For the first layer, use the longer pasta sheets to line the bottom and sides of the pan and allow some overhang on all sides.

Cover the first layer, and each subsequent one, with a few ladles of sauce, enough to cover the pasta, 4 - 6 cubes of butter, a light covering of bocconcini, a thin layer of mozzarella, and a sprinkle of grated parmesan.

Continue to boil the fresh pasta dough, as needed. For all remaining layers, cut and trim pasta sheets, with a knife or with hands, to accurately fit the pan. Continue and repeat the process, for as many layers as will fit, without overfilling. The more layers the better (we aim for 10 layers).

Use the overhanging pasta to complete the final layer. Carefully, fold over the overhanging strips, spreading sauce in between the folds to prevent sticking; close off the top with extra pasta strips, so as to cover or wrap the lasagna, like a gift.

Spread the top layer sparingly with sauce, just enough to moisten the layer, but not saturate it; sprinkle lightly with parmesan.

Cover in foil. Freeze until needed or bake right away.

When baking, place the baking pan on a cookie sheet, to prevent any spillage.

Bake, covered in foil, fresh or thawed, at 350°F (180°C) about 60 minutes or until sauce bubbles and cheese is melted. (A larger tray may take longer)

Remove foil, switch oven to broil and put lasagna back in for about 5 minutes,or enough to crisp up the top. Remove from the oven; loosely cover and allow to rest for 10 - 15 minutes before cutting and serving.

MANICOTTI AL
BURRO E LIMONE

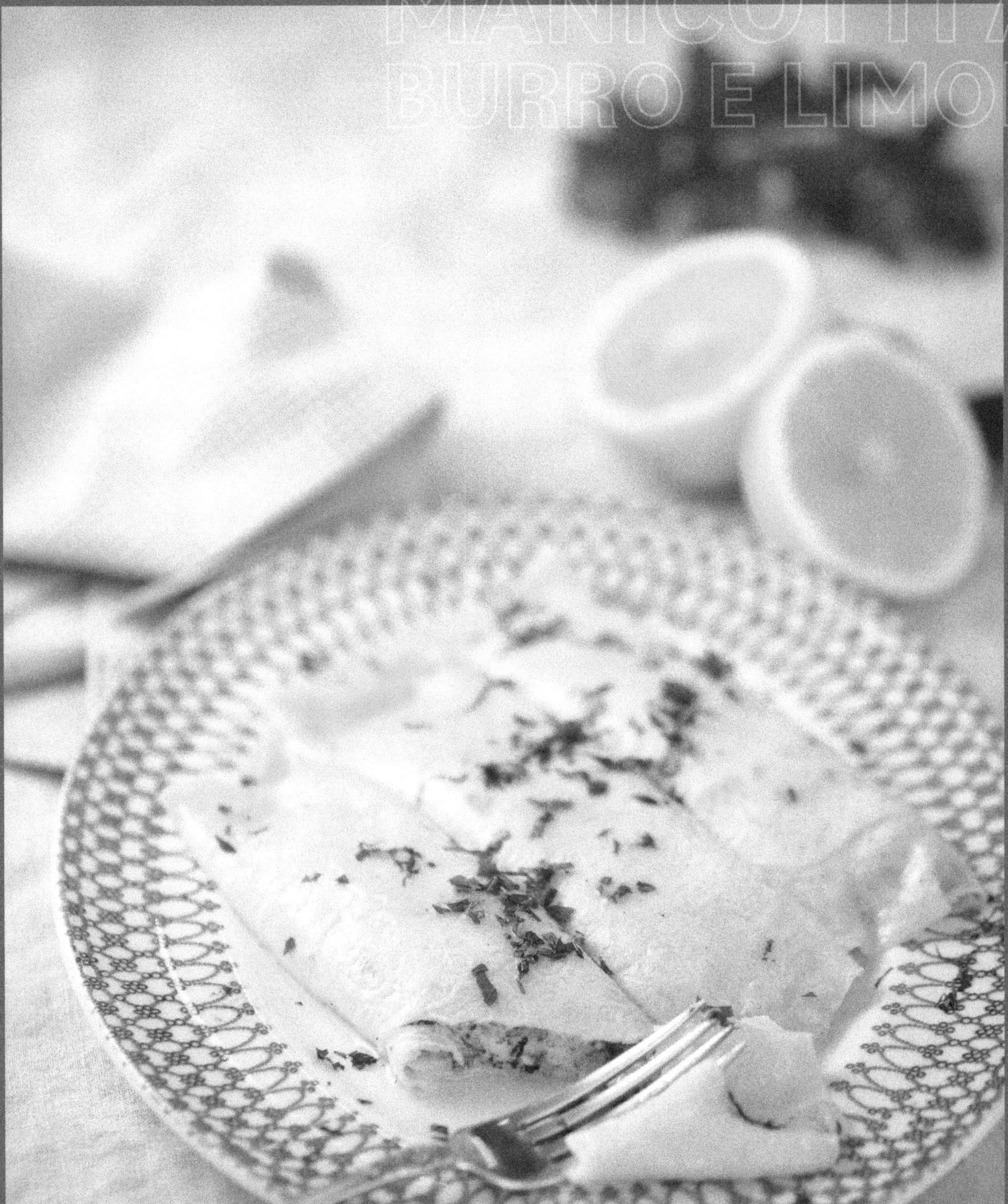

MANICOTTI AL BURRO E LIMONE

MANICOTTI WITH LEMON-BUTTER SAUCE

yields: 16-18 .... time: 90mins .... Advanced ....

Manicotti tubes are crepes, not pasta. Wait... what? These rolled crepes are filled with a cheesy, ricotta-spinach filling. Our smooth lemon-butter sauce will have you poppin' your lips in appreciation of the tangy sauce over the savoury tubes.

EQUIPMENT

Food Processor

STEP 1 INGREDIENTS

3 large eggs

¼ tsp. salt

2 cups water

1½ cups (210 g) all-purpose flour

2 Tbsp butter – for brushing pan

STEP 2 INGREDIENTS

500 g fresh whole ricotta, drained

2 Tbsp olive oil

1 green onion, finely chopped

1 garlic clove, minced

60 g thinly sliced prosciutto, finely chopped (optional)

225 g fresh spinach leaves

2 large eggs

¾ cup grated parmesan or pecorino

100 g mozzarella or bocconcini, shredded

2 Tbsp fresh parsley, finely minced

pinch of nutmeg

salt and pepper, to taste

STEP 1 – CREPES

DIRECTIONS

Whisk eggs, salt and water in a bowl. Add flour and mix to a smooth, thin, runny batter. Let stand for 30 minutes.

Heat a 20 cm (8-inch) non-stick crepe pan on medium-high heat. Brush pan with a dab of butter.

Lift the hot buttered pan from the heat and pour just under a quarter cup of batter into the center. Twirl pan to allow batter to swirl, stretch out and coat the base, as thinly and evenly as possible.

Cook until the bottom is set and the edges begin to separate from the pan, about 1 minute or less; flip crepe and cook another 30 seconds – enough for batter to set.

Transfer crepe to plate. Repeat with remaining batter, brushing the pan, lightly with butter, each time. Layer crepes between sheets of parchment paper. Wrap and refrigerate until ready to use.

STEP 2 – FILLING

DIRECTIONS

Wrap the ricotta in a cheesecloth and set in sieve to drain.

Finely chop prosciutto, if using.

In a large pan, heat oil on medium-high temperature. Sauté green onion and garlic until fragrant, about 2 minutes; add prosciutto and cook until softened, another minute. Add the spinach and sauté until wilted (3 - 5 minutes). Remove from heat. Drain in a sieve, as it cools, then squeeze-dry.

STEP 3 INGREDIENTS

2 Tbsp + 1 cup cold butter, cubed

2 shallots, finely minced

2 whole garlic cloves

2 cups white wine

juice of 2 lemons (½ cup), freshly squeezed and strained

½ tsp freshly ground salt and pepper

2 Tbsp of combined fresh herbs (parsley, thyme, basil), finely chopped

Place eggs, parmesan, mozzarella, parsley, drained ricotta and sautéed spinach in processor. Pulse several times until the mixture is combined and evenly blended. Season with salt, pepper and a pinch of nutmeg. Cover and refrigerate, 20 minutes.

In the meantime, prepare the lemon sauce.

STEP 3 – LEMON BUTTER SAUCE

DIRECTIONS
Squeeze and strain the lemon juice; set aside

In a non-stick pan, over medium heat, melt two tablespoons of butter. Add the shallots and garlic; cook and stir until softened and fragrant, about 2 - 3 minutes. Add the wine and lemon juice and bring to a boil over high heat. Continue to cook, over medium-high heat until liquid is reduced to half, about 7- 8 minutes.

Reduce heat to low; add several cubes of butter, at a time, swirling until the butter is melted. Allow the butter to slowly emulsify into a sauce. Continue adding tablespoons of butter, until all has been incorporated. Season with salt and pepper and remove sauce from heat.

Strain in a sieve for a smooth textured sauce (optional).

STEP 4 – ASSEMBLY

DIRECTIONS
Preheat oven to 350ºF (180ºC).

Generously butter a large baking dish.

Fill the crepes. Spoon 3 - 4 Tbsp of filling, across the top third of a crepe and roll to resemble a fat cigar; arrange seam side down in the baking dish. Repeat and arrange crepes in one layer.

Cover crepes with sauce. Bake, covered with foil, until sauce bubbles – about 20 - 30 minutes.

Garnish with herbs and serve.

MAMMA'S TIPS

Crepes can be prepared a day ahead. Wrap tightly and refrigerate, or freeze for up to 1 month, but bring to room temperature before using.

CHEF'S NOTES

Chapter 6

RICE, GNOCCHI AND POLENTA

GNOCCHI DI PATATE
CON FUNGHI E PANNA

POTATO GNOCCHI IN PORCINI SAUCE

serves: 4-6 ·········· time: 2hrs 30mins ············ Advanced ·····················

Often mistaken for pasta, gnocchi stands proud as Italy's answer to the dumpling. Little doughy lumps specifically formed to hold as much sauce as possible, both through absorption and exterior groove. Our creamy porcini ensures that it's the "fun" in funghi which tickles your tongue.

EQUIPMENT

Potato Ricer or Food Mill

STEP 1 INGREDIENTS

1 kg (about 5) Yukon gold
or russet potatoes

2 cups "00" all-purpose flour,
plus 1 - 1½ cups more for
kneading, shaping and dusting

½ cup grated parmesan

1 egg, lightly beaten

salt and pepper, to taste

pinch of nutmeg

STEP 1 – GNOCCHI

DIRECTIONS
Preheat oven to 400°F (200°C).

Pierce each potato with a fork several times, place directly on rack in the oven and bake for about 45 minutes or until tender right through, when pierced again with a fork.

Remove from oven, let cool long enough to handle, peel potatoes and press through a potato ricer or food mill into a bowl.

Add the grated parmesan, egg, salt, pepper and nutmeg. Sprinkle with 1 cup of flour and mix to combine.

Gather up the shaggy potato mass, pat into a loose ball and transfer onto a well-floured work area.

Using a scraper or hands, incorporate the flour into the potatoes to form a workable dough. Flatten dough, fold in half and press down.

Repeat the process of folding and pressing, until a uniform dough comes together.

Lightly knead, sprinkling extra flour, as needed until the dough is smooth, pliable and not sticky.

With a knife or scraper, cut the dough into a workable wedge or section.

Flour hands and roll out each piece into a rope-like segment, about the thickness of a finger.

Cut each rope into approx. 2 cm pieces. To create ridges, use a gnocchi paddle or a fork. With the tines of a fork facing down and

STEP 2 INGREDIENTS

4 Tbsp olive oil

2 garlic cloves, finely minced

1 shallot, finely chopped

500 g fresh porcini or other
mushrooms, chopped or sliced

1 tsp fresh or ½ tsp dried thyme

salt and pepper, to taste

¾ cup white wine

1½ cup cream

2 Tbsp butter

2 Tbsp chopped parsley

1½ cup reserved cooking water

freshly grated parmesan

away from you, press each gnocchi piece, in quick motion, up along the fork, then let it fall back down.

This will leave the indentation of the tines on one side and the depression of your finger on the other.

Place the gnocchi on a cookie sheet, lightly dusted with flour or cornmeal. Use right away or refrigerate uncovered until needed. If freezing, freeze first on the floured cookie sheets (without overlapping); then, store in freezer bags. One generous serving is based on about 30 - 35 gnocchi.

STEP 2 – PORCINI SAUCE

DIRECTIONS

In a large pan, heat oil, on medium-high heat, add the garlic and cook until fragrant, but not browned, 30 seconds.

Add shallots and sauté until soft and translucent, about 5 minutes.

Add mushrooms; season with thyme, salt and pepper and sauté until juices evaporate and mushrooms are golden, about 10 minutes.

Add wine and cook until mostly evaporated and mushrooms are tender, about 4 - 6 minutes.

Add the cream and half the parsley; bring to a rolling simmer and stir until combined and creamy, 2 minutes. Add butter, reduce heat to low or set aside until gnocchi are ready.

Bring a large pot of salted water to a boil. Add the gnocchi (in batches, if too crowded in pot) and cook until they float, 2 - 3 minutes.

Reserve about 1½ cup of gnocchi-cooking water.

With a slotted spoon, transfer the cooked gnocchi directly into the sauce. Gently, toss and coat gnocchi, while adding some of the cooking water, as needed, to keep the gnocchi glossy and the sauce smooth and fluid.

Garnish with parsley and serve with grated parmesan.

SPINACH-RICOTTA GNOCCHI IN GORGONZOLA SAUCE

serves: 4-6 .... time: 2hrs 30mins .... Advanced ....

As one of the oldest Italian foods, gnocchi are known by many names. Malfatti (badly made), ravioli nudi (naked ravioli), or in this case, topini verdi (little green mice). Because these spinach-ricotta gnocchi are lighter than their potato counterparts, we've gone ahead and paired them with a rich gorgonzola sauce.

EQUIPMENT

Food Processor

STEP 1 INGREDIENTS

300 g fresh spinach

500 g fresh firm ricotta, drained

1 egg, slightly beaten

½ cup freshly grated parmesan

salt and pepper, to taste

pinch of nutmeg

2 cups (280 g) all-purpose flour plus 1 - 1½ cups more, for kneading, shaping and dusting.

STEP 1 - GNOCCHI

DIRECTIONS

Blanch spinach in boiling salted water for 1 minute. Drain.

When cool to the touch, drain and press the excess liquid from the spinach, wrap in a cheesecloth and squeeze-dry to release all moisture. Purée in a processor and place in a large mixing bowl.

Drain the ricotta in a strainer and press down to release excess moisture.

Add the ricotta, egg, parmesan, salt, pepper and a pinch of nutmeg to the spinach. Mix to combine.

Sprinkle about half a cup of flour over the mixture and mix to incorporate (dough will be sticky). Transfer onto a well- floured work area and sprinkle more flour on top of mixture. Using a scraper, continue to add and integrate the flour by cutting, folding and pressing the dough many times, until the mixture begins to hold together as a ball and can be worked, by hand. Flour hands and work area and begin to knead lightly, until the dough becomes smooth, pliable and not sticky to touch.

Cut a small section of dough. With a light touch, roll the dough with both hands, in a back and forth motion, starting at the center and stretching it out to form a rope, the width of a finger. Have just enough flour on the board, or on your fingers, to keep dough from sticking (too much flour will make rolling difficult).

Cut rope into individual bite-sized gnocchi, about 2 cm long. To

STEP 2 INGREDIENTS

2 Tbsp butter

1½ cup cream

200 g sweet gorgonzola cheese, rind removed, cut into small cubes

salt and pepper to taste

dash of cayenne (optional)

1½ cups reserved cooking water

2 Tbsp fresh chopped parsley

grated parmesan, for serving

create ridges, use a gnocchi paddle or a fork. With the tines of a fork facing down and away from you, press each gnocchi piece, in quick motion, up along the fork, then let it fall back down. This will leave the indentation of the tines on one side and the depression of your finger, on the other.

Place gnocchi on a cookie sheet, dusted with flour or cornmeal, without overlapping. Cook right away or refrigerate uncovered, until needed. If freezing, freeze first on the floured cookie sheets, then, store in freezer bags. One generous serving is based on about 30 - 35 gnocchi.

When ready to cook, bring a large pot of salted water to a boil, and begin making the sauce.

STEP 2 - MAKE THE SAUCE AND COOK GNOCCHI

DIRECTIONS

In a large pan, melt the butter on medium-high heat. Add cream and cook until small bubbles form, about 1 minute. Add the crumbled gorgonzola and cook until melted. Reduce heat and season to taste with salt, pepper and cayenne.

Cook gnocchi in boiling salted water (in batches, if too crowded in pot), until they float, 2 - 3 minutes.

Set aside about 1½ cup of the gnocchi-cooking water.

With a slotted spoon, transfer the cooked gnocchi directly into the sauce.

Gently, toss and coat the gnocchi with the sauce. Gradually, add as much of the gnocchi-cooking water as needed, to keep the gnocchi glossy and the sauce smooth and fluid. Garnish with parsley and serve with grated parmesan.

RISOTTO ALLA MILANESE

serves: 4-6 .... time: 30mins ....

The ideal conditions of the Lombardy region, surrounding Milan, make this area one of Europe's more prominent producers of rice. It's no wonder that this sweet, floral, creamy risotto, made golden by the inclusion of saffron, has become one of Italy's most popular rice dishes. If you can only make one risotto, make it this one!

INGREDIENTS

8 cups chicken broth, refer to page 206 in the BASICS chapter for broth recipe

½ tsp (8 - 10) saffron threads

4 Tbsp butter or olive oil

1 onion, finely chopped

2 cups arborio or carnaroli rice

1 cup white wine

salt and pepper, to taste

2 Tbsp butter

½ cup grated parmesan

DIRECTIONS

Heat the broth. Place the saffron threads in a cup; crush and break up with a teaspoon, pour half a cup of warm broth over the saffron and set aside to dissolve.

In a large pot, heat butter or oil, over medium heat and sauté the onion, until soft and translucent, about 5 - 6 minutes.

Add the rice and stir to coat. Cook 3 - 4 minutes until the edges of the rice become translucent.

Pour in wine and stir and cook until evaporated.

Season with salt and pepper.

Over medium heat, add warm broth, about 1 cup at a time, stirring frequently; gradually add more broth whenever the liquid is absorbed.

Cook and continue to stir for about 16 - 20 minutes until the rice is creamy and al dente, adding more broth, as needed. Add the saffron mixture, washing down the cup with more broth to retain all of the spice's golden colour, and allow it to absorb into the risotto.

When the risotto is very creamy but still fluid, stir in butter and half the parmesan cheese. Serve and sprinkle with remaining cheese.

MAMMA'S TIPS

Make your own broth!
Refer to Brodo recipe on page 206.
It's always good to have on hand.

ARANCINI WITH HAM AND CHEESE

yields: 22-24 .... time: 3hrs .... Advanced ....

In Palermo it's called "Arancina" and it's round like an orange. In Catania, it's an "Arancino" and it's cone-shaped, like the volcano, Etna! Regardless of shape, enjoy the mouth explosion that comes from these delicious cheese and ham filled crispy golden rice balls.

STEP 2 INGREDIENTS

4 cups water

4 cups chicken broth

½ tsp (8 - 10) saffron threads (or powdered)

4 cups arborio or carnaroli rice

2 Tbsp butter

salt and pepper, to taste

4 beaten egg yolks (reserve whites)

¾ cup freshly grated parmesan cheese

2 Tbsp finely chopped parsley

¼ tsp ground nutmeg

STEP 1 - BÉCHAMEL SAUCE AND BROTH

DIRECTIONS
Refer to page 205 in the BASICS chapter for Béchamel recipe.

Refer to page 206 in the BASICS chapter for Brodo recipe.

Prepare and set aside.

STEP 2 - PREPARE THE RICE

DIRECTIONS
In a large pot, bring water and broth to a boil.

Scoop a ladle of the boiling liquid into a cup, stir in the saffron threads, crush or break down with a teaspoon and allow to dissolve.

Add rice to the pot; stir and season well with salt.

Cook covered, over medium heat, until liquid is absorbed and rice is cooked (15 - 18 minutes). Add the saffron liquid about 10 minutes into the cooking (rinse cup with an extra half cup of water or broth and add to rice. When rice is cooked (al dente) but still fluid, add the butter, stir to combine, adjust seasoning with salt and pepper and remove from heat.

Spread the rice onto a large shallow platter to cool. When completely cooled, add the grated parmesan, 4 beaten egg yolks, parsley and nutmeg. Mix ingredients together, well.

Set aside and move to Step 3.

MAMMA'S TIPS

Freeze in the breaded stage and deep-fry, 7 - 8 minutes from frozen, less if thawed.

STEP 3 INGREDIENTS

1 cup prepared béchamel
sauce

125 g mozzarella, provoletta or
other semi-soft cheese, diced
into small cubes

75 ml (⅓ cup) butter, in cubes
of about ½ tsp equivalent

75 g black forest ham, outer
skin removed, finely diced

STEP 4 INGREDIENTS

4 beaten egg whites

2 cups dry breadcrumbs,
in a bowl

2 L sunflower or vegetable oil
for frying

STEP 3 - SHAPING THE BALLS

DIRECTIONS

Line a large baking sheet with parchment. Have all of the filling ingredients ready.

When shaping arancini, hands will get sticky and will need to be washed and dried every so often. To reduce the stickiness, pour some olive oil in a small bowl and rub a few drops onto your hands, when necessary. Latex gloves also help.

Scoop about ¼ cup of rice and flatten, not too thinly, onto your cupped hand.

Fill the center of the cupped rice with 1 rounded tsp of béchamel sauce, about 3 - 4 cubes (2 tsp) of cheese, ½ tsp butter and ½ tsp diced ham. (Preparing clusters of cheese, butter and ham cubes, before starting, may simplify the process and achieve uniformity). Close the rice around the filling, top with more rice to encase the filling completely and shape into small "orange-sized" balls.

Set on the parchment-lined tray, until all arancini are shaped.

Refrigerate for 30 minutes.

STEP 4 - COATING AND FRYING THE BALLS

DIRECTIONS

Whisk egg whites in one bowl and add breadcrumbs to another bowl.

Using a brush or your hand, coat each rice ball with the beaten egg white, then roll in breadcrumbs (wet hand / dry hand method, if working alone).

Fry in a deep fryer or in a heavy pot with oil, on medium-high heat, between 350°F(180°C) - 375°F(190°C) for 3 - 5 minutes, until crisp and golden.

Drain on paper towels.

Serve hot, on its own, or with our basic tomato sauce.

Refer to page 198 in the BASICS chapter for Basic Tomato Sauce recipe.

MAMMA'S TIPS

Bake instead of frying. With hands, coat breaded rice ball with oil; place on a greased pan. Bake at 425°F (220°C) for 20 - 30 minutes or until golden. If frozen, thaw for about 1 hour; re-bread if required; coat with oil and bake in the same way.

STEF SAYS

Enjoy the classic filling or change-it-up.
Make it yours, fill it with anything that
makes you happy... and fits. Why not
change the shape? Oval? Cone?

2 - 3 cubes of cheese
½ tsp butter
1 tsp béchamel
1 tsp of chopped
sautéed mushrooms.

2 - 3 cubes of cheese
½ tsp butter
1 rounded tsp of bolognese or
basic tomato sauce
½ tsp cooked peas

POLENTA WITH PORK SAUSAGE

serves: 6-8 .... time: 1hr ....

Polenta's lean cornmeal goodness acts as a natural base to complement meat or tomato sauces, grilled or sauteed vegetable toppings or the succulent fatty nuggets of an uncased sausage that gloriously crowns this dish. Along with a salad, it makes for a substantial and hearty meal.

STEP 1 INGREDIENTS

900 g (6 - 7 links) pork sausage, casings removed

4 Tbsp olive oil

1 onion, finely chopped

500 g fresh cremini or mixed mushrooms, sliced

1 cup dry red wine

500 ml (2 cups) canned diced tomatoes, undrained

1 cup water

2 Tbsp tomato paste

salt and pepper, to taste

STEP 2 INGREDIENTS

8 cups salted water

2 cups cornmeal (polenta)

2 Tbsp (30 g) butter

2 Tbsp (30 g) crumbled goat cheese (optional)

¼ cup grated parmesan cheese + more for serving

½ tsp ground pepper

STEP 1 – SAUCE

DIRECTIONS

Heat oil in a large saucepan, at medium-high heat.

Add onion and sauté, until softened, about 5 minutes. Coarsely mash the sausage, with a fork, then add it to the onions. With a wooden spoon, turn and continue to break down the sausage as it browns evenly, 8 - 10 minutes.

Add the mushrooms; stir and cook until their juices have evaporated and mushrooms are soft and browned, another 8 - 10 minutes.

Increase heat and add wine; bring to a boil and cook down until mixture is glossy and well coated, 2 - 3 minutes.

Add the tomatoes, water and tomato paste. Season with salt and pepper.

Bring to a boil then reduce heat to medium-low. Cook, with lid ajar, until liquid has absorbed and lightly thickened, about 30 minutes; stir occasionally.

Remove from heat until ready to use.

STEP 2 – POLENTA

DIRECTIONS

Place salted water in a large, heavy pot, over high heat. As the water heats, pour the cornmeal in a thin, consistent, stream; stir to prevent lumps.

As the water comes to a boil, reduce heat to medium or medium-low and continue stirring, for about 30 minutes. If the heat is too high, the polenta will squirt. Polenta is cooked when it begins to separate from the sides of the pot.

When cooked, stir in the butter, goat cheese (optional) and parmesan and mix to combine. Remove from heat and serve with the sausage mixture in one of two ways:

1 – Spread the hot polenta evenly onto plates, spoon sausage mixture over polenta and serve with freshly grated cheese and, if you like it hot, a sprinkle of hot chilli pepper flakes.

2 – Preheat oven to 400°F (205°C). Pour the cooked polenta in a large buttered baking dish; spread sausage mixture over top, sprinkle with grated parmesan and bake, uncovered in the oven, until hot and bubbly, 10 - 15 minutes.

Remove from the oven, allow to rest for 5 minutes, then cut into individual servings.

Serve, to your liking, with extra grated parmesan and/or hot chilli pepper flakes.

MAMMA'S TIPS

When making the polenta, add a flavour boost! Instead of water, use broth (*Brodo) or half of each (water + brodo). *Refer to page 206 in the BASICS chapter for Brodo recipe.

CHEF'S NOTES

Chapter 7

MEAT, CHICKEN, AND FISH

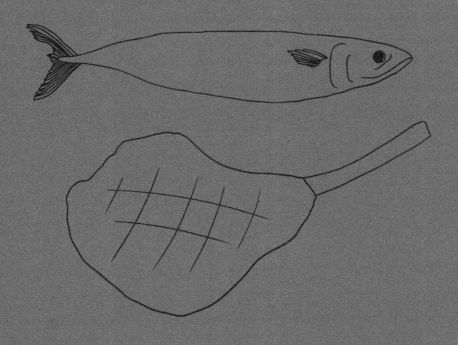

PICCATA DI
POLLO AL LIMONE

CHICKEN PICCATA

serves: 4-5 .... time: 45mins ....

Thin and tender chicken escalopes dredged, fried and simmered in a sauce of lemon, white wine and capers. This easy to prepare dish is sure to become a part of your home cooking repertoire as it ticks all the boxes: easy, very palatable, substantial, delicious. You gotta Piccata!

INGREDIENTS

2 lemons (1½ sliced - ½ juiced)

¼ cup capers, rinsed and drained

1½ cup chicken broth

¼ tsp hot chilli flakes (optional)

2 Tbsp finely chopped fresh parsley

½ cup flour

salt and pepper, to taste

4 skinless boneless chicken breast halves

6 - 8 Tbsp olive oil, as needed

6 Tbsp butter, as needed

1 whole garlic clove, halved

¾ cup dry white wine

DIRECTIONS

Juice half a lemon and strain into a 2-cup bowl; slice remaining lemon into thin slices; set aside.

Add rinsed capers, chicken broth and chilli flakes (optional) to the lemon juice; set aside. Finely chop parsley and set aside. Place flour in a shallow bowl and season with salt and pepper.

Butterfly or fillet chicken breast halves each into two or three slices. Cover with cellophane and lightly pound to an even thickness. Generously season with salt and pepper.

In a large pan, on medium-high heat, add 2 Tbsp each of olive oil and butter. Add the lemon slices and cook, about 2 minutes on each side, until the slices begin to caramelize and turn golden. Remove from pan and set aside.

Reheat pan, on medium-high heat, with 2 Tbsp of olive oil. Dredge chicken with flour, shake off any excess and pan-fry, in batches, until each side is golden or lightly browned, about 3 - 4 minutes per side. Transfer to a plate and keep warm. Continue with remaining chicken, adding oil, as needed.

Add the garlic halves and the wine; deglaze while scraping off the pan. Add the capers, lemon juice, broth and chilli flakes. Bring liquid to a boil and cook, until slightly reduced, 3 - 5 minutes.

Lower heat to medium; swirl in the remaining butter; add the parsley and return the lemon slices and chicken to the pan; reheat in the simmering sauce, turning several times until the chicken is hot again and well coated, 2 minutes. Remove garlic pieces.

Spoon sauce and lemon slices, (delicious to eat) over chicken and serve. For a complete meal, serve with pasta or rice and your favourite vegetable.

NONNA'S MEATBALLS

yields: 18-20 .... time: 2hrs + basic tomato sauce ....

The secret to these tasty super soft meatballs is in the number of eggs. Dad would immediately know if Mamma reduced the recipe by an egg or two. As such, they earned the moniker "eggballs". Despite poking some fun, Nonna's meatballs are legit treasures, and you'll be hailed as a hero for nailing these incredible saucy-soaked balls. This recipe will yield 18 - 20 meatballs and plenty of sauce to serve with your favourite pasta.

INGREDIENTS

250 g lean minced beef

250 g minced pork

1 garlic clove, minced

1 green onion, finely chopped

2 Tbsp fresh parsley, finely chopped

1 tsp oregano

salt and pepper to taste

½ tsp chilli pepper flakes, or to taste

¼ tsp ground nutmeg

6 eggs

½ cup grated parmesan cheese

½ - ¾ cup dried breadcrumbs

4 Tbsp olive oil, for browning meatballs.

DIRECTIONS

Place minced meat in a large bowl; add garlic, onion, seasonings and herbs. In a separate bowl whisk together eggs, then add to meat mixture. Mix to combine the eggs with the meat. It will be very liquid. Add the grated cheese and ½ cup of breadcrumbs. Mix uniformly with a spatula. The consistency will be soft but should still bind together. Refrigerate for at least 20 minutes.

In the meantime, begin making the sauce, and allow it to simmer on low heat.

Refer to page 198 in the BASICS chapter for Basic Tomato Sauce recipe.

Remove mixture from refrigerator. If mixture is too moist for shaping, mix in remainder of breadcrumbs. Roll well and shape into meatballs (billiard ball size).

Add oil to pan and brown meatballs in batches, over medium-high heat. Turn over, gently, to brown all sides; transfer to a plate, lined with paper towels to drain off fat.

Carefully, drop meatballs into sauce. Cover and simmer over low heat, stirring occasionally for 40 - 50 minutes.

When cooked, remove meatballs from sauce with a slotted spoon onto a platter.

If cooking pasta, bring salted water to a boil; add pasta, cook; drain; toss with sauce. Sprinkle with grated cheese. Serve with meatballs on top.

STEF SAYS

Make it a sandwich! Load finished meatballs onto a soft bread roll and cover with a thin slice of provolone and a generous ladle of warm sauce over top. Dig in, and try to keep your shirt clean.

VEAL MARSALA

serves: 4-6 .... time: 40mins ....

Marsala, a renowned, fortified wine and key ingredient in this veal dish, gets its name from the town of the same name, in Sicily. This dish serves up tender pan-fried veal escalopes, paired with thin sliced mushrooms that soak up the nutty caramelized flavour of the rich, bronzed sauce.

INGREDIENTS

1 Kg veal slices 1 cm (escalopes), (top round)

¾ cup flour

salt and pepper, to taste

6 - 8 Tbsp olive oil

500 g mushrooms, sliced

2 tsp freshly chopped thyme

1 cup dry Marsala wine

2 cups beef broth

¾ cup heavy cream

2 Tbsp butter

1 Tbsp freshly chopped parsley

DIRECTIONS

Place cellophane over the veal and lightly pound and stretch the escalopes with a cleaver to an even thinness; season with salt and pepper.

Place flour in a shallow dish. Remove 1 Tbsp of the measured flour and add it to 1 cup of the beef broth; whisk and set aside for later.

In a large pan, heat 2 Tbsp olive oil, over medium-high heat; lightly dredge the veal slices with the flour and, in batches, sear veal slices, about 1 minute on each side. Remove from pan and set aside. Repeat, adding 1 or 2 Tbsp of olive oil with each new batch.

In the same pan, add 2 more Tbsp of olive oil and sauté the mushrooms. Season with fresh thyme, salt and pepper. Cook on high heat until their juices are absorbed and the mushrooms are a golden brown, about 7 - 8 minutes. Remove mushrooms from the pan and set aside.

With the pan on high heat, add the Marsala and bring to a rolling sizzle. Whisk in the broth and flour mixture, stir until slightly thickened, then add the remaining broth. Bring to a boil, lower heat to medium and simmer until liquid reduces slightly and sauce begins to thicken, 5 - 7 minutes. Add cream and stir to combine; season with salt and pepper and swirl in the butter.

Return veal and mushrooms to the simmering sauce. Gently coat the veal and mushrooms with the sauce.

Plate and spoon sauce over the veal; garnish with parsley, serve and enjoy.

BRAISED BEEF ROLLS IN TOMATO SAUCE

yields: 12 ·········· time: 4hrs + basic tomato sauce ············ Advanced ··············

Tender beef stuffed full of goodness, braised and slow-cooked in homemade tomato sauce for hours. These Sicilian-style flavour bombs absorb the sauce in the meat and stuffing alike and, with the generous sauce allotment, they pair well with pasta, polenta or rice, on the side.

EQUIPMENT

Baking Dish

STEP 1 INGREDIENTS

¼ cup pine nuts, toasted

1 cup milk

3 cups (100 g) small bread cubes, from day-old bread, crust removed (approx. 4 slices)

1 clove garlic, crushed

¼ cup finely chopped fresh Italian parsley

1 tsp each chopped fresh rosemary and thyme

¼ cup golden raisins

½ cup freshly grated parmesan

80 - 100g provolone, shredded or cut into 12 thin strips or slices

salt and freshly ground black pepper

STEP 1 – STUFFING

DIRECTIONS

Toast pine nuts, on medium heat, in a dry pan on stove-top, stirring frequently until golden, 4 - 5 minutes; remove from heat and set aside.

Soak the bread cubes in the milk, for about 15 minutes, or until softened.

Finely mince together the garlic, parsley, rosemary and thyme and place in a medium bowl. Roughly chop the pine nuts and raisins and add to the mixture; add the grated parmesan and shredded provolone. If the provolone is cut into strips or slices, don't add it to the mixture. Instead, place it separately on the beef along with the prosciutto and stuffing when assembling the rolls in Step 2 (next page).

Drain, squeeze and discard any excess milk from the bread and add to the ingredients in the bowl. Season with salt and pepper. Mix to combine.

MAMMA'S TIPS

This dish can be cooked completely on the stove-top. Add beef rolls to the sauce after the tomatoes, water and seasonings come to a boil. If needed, add more water to keep the beef rolls completely submerged. Cover and simmer, 2 - 3 hours, until the beef is tender, checking, stirring, and turning every 15 - 20 minutes.

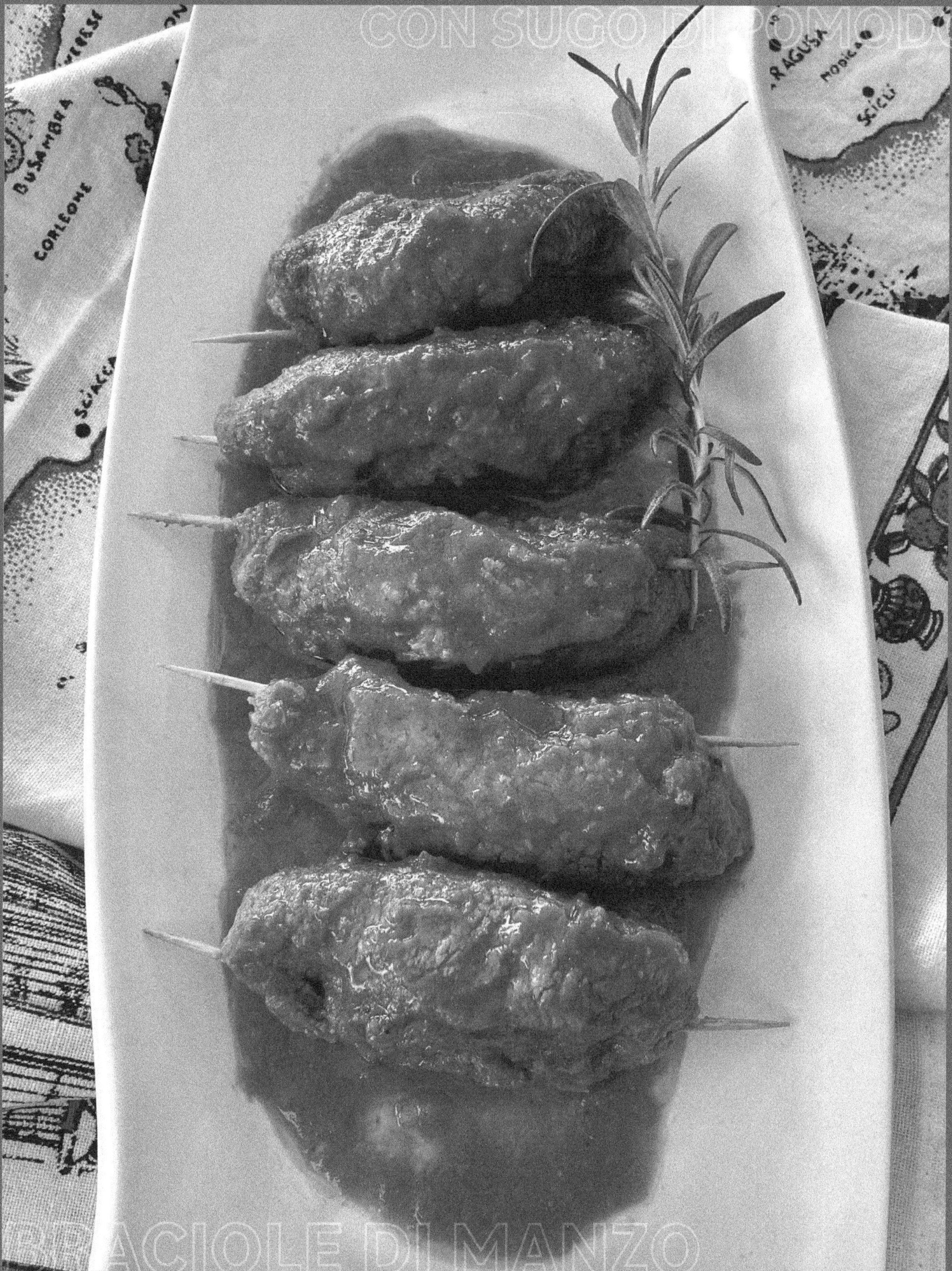

STEP 2 INGREDIENTS

1 Kg beef top sirloin, cut into
12 thin slices

12 slices Italian prosciutto

4 Tbsp olive oil, for browning

STEP 2 – MEAT PREP AND ASSEMBLY

DIRECTIONS

Pound the beef slices to thin even slices, less than 1cm thick.
Season with salt and pepper.

Spread about 1 Tbsp of filling over each beef slice, leaving the
edges clear; place a slice of prosciutto over the filling.

Roll the beef into a cylinder, tucking in the sides to hold in the filling,
as you roll. Secure with toothpicks or tie with twine. Repeat until all
rolls are completed.

Heat olive oil in a large Dutch oven over medium-high heat. Place
the rolls, seam side down and sear.

Turn the rolls so that all sides are browned. Remove from the pot
and set aside.

STEP 3 – SAUCE AND COOKING

DIRECTIONS

Refer to page 198 in the BASICS chapter for Basic Tomato Sauce
recipe.

Preheat oven to 325 °F (165 °C).

In the same pot, make the sauce. When the sauce comes to a boil,
return beef rolls to the pot, making sure that they are completely
submerged; if not, add enough water to keep the rolls covered.

Cover, place in the oven and bake, for 2 - 3 hours or until beef rolls
are tender and easily pierced by a fork, checking and turning rolls
once or twice during the baking time.

Carefully remove the toothpicks or twine before serving.

MAMMA'S TIPS

Prepare up to 2 days in advance – stuff
and roll the beef, sear, place in the pot
with sauce and refrigerate until ready to
cook or bake.

OSSOBUCO

serves: 4 time: 3hrs 30mins

Ossobuco literally translates to "bone hole". It references the marrow that resides in said hole and which cooks into a heavenly dollop of gelatinous flavour. The cross-cut veal shanks are braised then baked in white wine, broth, pulsed vegetables and finished with a tart gremolata. Accompanied with a risotto Milanese, your troubles will be forgotten for the span of your meal.

EQUIPMENT

Dutch Oven

Processor

INGREDIENTS

4 cross-cut veal shanks, each about 5 cm (2 in) thick

salt and freshly ground pepper

½ cup flour, for dredging

30 g butter + 30 ml olive oil (approx.)

1 garlic clove, smashed

1 onion, chopped

1 carrot, diced

1 celery stalk, diced

1 cup dry white wine

2 - 3 cups chicken broth (enough to submerge the ossobuco)

1 bay leaf

1 sprig of thyme

GREMOLATA INGREDIENTS

2 Tbsp (30 ml) finely chopped fresh parsley,
zest of 1 lemon
1 garlic clove
1 anchovy fillet

DIRECTIONS

Preheat oven to 325°F (165°C).

Pat dry veal shanks with paper towels; secure shanks to the bone with kitchen twine, if you wish. The meat may otherwise fall from the bone.

Season shanks with salt and pepper and dredge in flour; shake off excess.

In a large Dutch oven pot, heat butter and oil; add shanks to the hot pot and brown well, 2 - 3 minutes on each side; carefully remove browned shanks and set aside.

Roughly pulse the onion, garlic, carrot and celery, in a processor and add to the same pot as used to brown shanks.

Sauté until soft and translucent, about 6 - 8 minutes.

Add the wine and cook over high heat for 3 - 4 minutes. Return shanks to the pot.

Pour in the broth; add bay leaf and thyme sprig. Cover the pot and place in the center of oven; bake for 2 ½ - 3 hours or until meat is falling off the bone.

Meanwhile, prepare the gremolata by combining the parsley, lemon rind, garlic clove and anchovy on a board and chopping them together very finely; set aside in a small bowl.

When cooked, remove bayleaf from pot; cut off and discard twine; taste sauce for seasoning. Stir ¾ of the gremolata into the sauce, reserving the remainder for garnish. Keep covered and return to oven for another 10 minutes.

Carefully transfer shanks to a deep serving platter; pour sauce over the shanks and garnish with remaining gremolata.

Serve hot with bread, risotto, polenta or potatoes.

STEF SAYS

Meat butter makes it better! No matter what you serve your ossobuco with, ensure there is fresh toasted bread to spread the bone marrow over, it's the unique joy of this dish. The marrow transfers all of the meaty flavours of this dish to all that it touches.

ROAST PORK TENDERLOIN

serves: 6-8 .... time: 1hr ....

A prime cut of pork seasoned and rubbed to make a succulent dinner option with a sweet and fruity contrast. It stands up impeccably next to roasted potatoes, dark greens or your favourite light rice dish.

EQUIPMENT
Baking Dish

INGREDIENTS

2 pork tenderloins
(each about 375 g)

2 cloves garlic, each cut into
3 - 4 slivers

1 Tbsp fresh rosemary leaves, chopped

1 tsp each of salt, ground pepper, paprika, dried sage or thyme

2 Tbsp olive oil

4 apples, peeled, cored and each cut into 5 slices

juice of half a lemon

2 Tbsp butter

1 cup wine

½ cup balsamic vinegar

¼ cup maple syrup or honey

DIRECTIONS

In a small bowl, combine salt, pepper, paprika, sage or thyme. Trim and discard fat and film from tenderloins; place pork in a dish.

Make 3 - 4 slits in each tenderloin and fill with slivers of garlic and chopped rosemary. Brush each tenderloin with 1 tsp of olive oil; rub and press the dried seasoning mix over the tenderloins. Set aside.

Peel, core and slice apples; place in a bowl and sprinkle with lemon juice.

In a large pan, on medium-high heat, heat 1 Tbsp of butter for each batch and brown apple slices so that each side is golden but still firm, about 2 minutes on each side. Transfer apples to a large baking dish that will also be used for the tenderloins.

In the same pan, on medium-high heat, sear and brown the seasoned tenderloins, turning in thirds, about 3 minutes on each side. Transfer to the baking dish with the apples and set side by side.

Preheat oven to 400°F (200°C)

Using the same pan, again, on medium-high heat, add the wine, balsamic vinegar and maple syrup or honey; bring to a boil and cook down about 2 minutes until slightly reduced. Stir in 2 Tbsp butter, remove from heat and pour over the tenderloins and apples.

Cover the baking dish with foil and bake for 20 minutes or until internal temperature reaches 145°F (68°C). The pork should have a tinge of pink in the center. Remove from oven; cover loosely in foil and rest for 5 minutes.

Slice pork into 2 cm slices; arrange apples in between pork slices; strain juices from pan and drizzle over pork and apples. Garnish with fresh rosemary sprigs and serve.

BACCALÀ IN GUAZZETTO

serves: 4-6 .... time: 1hr + soaking time (3 days) ....

A Roman rendition of dried salt cod in a sauce of tomatoes and olives, speckled with pine nuts and golden raisins, which lend an unexpected sweetness to the dish.

INGREDIENTS

1 Kg thick dried salted cod (baccalà)

¾ cup flour

4 Tbsp olive oil

3 garlic cloves, crushed

1 cup white wine

800 ml can whole peeled plum tomatoes

1 cup of water

30 (1 cup) pitted whole black olives, drained

¼ cup golden raisins

¼ cup toasted pine nuts + some for garnish

salt and pepper, to taste

a sprig of parsley, finely minced

DIRECTIONS

Cut the salted cod (baccalà) into a few pieces. Soak in a large bowl filled with cold water, cover with cellophane and refrigerate for 3 days, changing the water twice daily.

Toast pine nuts, on medium heat, in a dry pan on stove-top, stirring frequently until golden, 4 - 5 minutes; remove from heat and set aside.

When ready to cook, drain the desalted baccalà and pat-dry. With your fingers, pull apart and separate the white skin from the flesh and remove any visible bones.

Cut baccalà into serving pieces, season with pepper and dredge lightly in flour.

Heat 4 Tbsp olive oil in a large pan, on medium-high heat. Fry until golden and crisp on both sides; drain on paper towels and set aside. Use the same pan to make the sauce.

Pour the canned plum tomatoes in a bowl and roughly crush and break down the tomatoes, with your hands or a wooden spoon; rinse the can with the cup of water.

In pan, sauté garlic until fragrant. Add the wine, deglaze and cook on high heat until evaporated. Add the tomatoes and the water. Bring to a boil, reduce heat to medium-low and simmer for 10 - 15 minutes. Add the olives, raisins and pine nuts. Season with salt and pepper.

Add the fried baccalà pieces, gently coating them into the sauce. Cook over medium-low heat, for about 10 minutes or until cod is tender, sauce has thickened and the flavours have blended.

Garnish and serve hot with extra pine nuts and chopped parsley.

MAMMA'S TIPS

Place the fried cod and sauce in a baking dish, cover and bake, in a preheated oven, at 350°F (180°C) for the last 10 minutes or until hot and ready to serve. For a lighter guazzetto, omit the flour dredging and proceed directly from patting-dry the cod, to frying.

BACCALÀ CON PATATE AL FREDDO

serves: 6-8 .... time: 40mins + soaking time (3 days) ....

A Christmas Eve tradition, this light and refreshing cold salad has all the necessary elements to transform into a spring or summer table pleaser whenever you can get your hands on salted cod.

INGREDIENTS

1 Kg thick dried salted cod (baccalà)

2 whole garlic cloves

2 bay leaves

1 Tbsp peppercorns

½ lemon, cut into 4 wedges

juice of ½ lemon

4 Tbsp olive oil

4 large potatoes

3 - 4 Tbsp white wine vinegar

salt and pepper, to taste

¼ tsp crushed hot chilli flakes, or to taste

2 Tbsp finely chopped parsley

DRESSING INGREDIENTS:

4 Tbsp olive oil

juice of ½ lemon

1 tsp Dijon mustard

2 garlic cloves, minced

salt and pepper, to taste

DIRECTIONS

Cut the salted cod (baccalà) into a few pieces. Soak in a large bowl filled with cold water, cover with cellophane and refrigerate for 3 days, changing the water twice daily.

Drain the desalted cod. Transfer to a large pot of water, seasoned with garlic cloves, bay leaves, peppercorns and lemon wedges and place on stove-top.

Bring to a simmer, and poach over medium heat, for 8 - 10 minutes or until the cod becomes opaque and begins to separate and flake. Remove from heat and, with a slotted spoon, gently transfer the cod to a platter to cool. (Boiling will toughen cod)

Separate the cod into flakes or slices, removing any skin or bones. Coat with about 4 Tbsp olive oil and lemon juice, cover and set aside.

Cook unpeeled potatoes in salted boiling water, about 20 minutes or until tender in centre. Let cool, then peel and cut into slices or chunks. Drizzle with vinegar, coat with about 3 Tbsp olive oil, season with salt and pepper and lightly toss.

Carefully combine the cod and potatoes and add dressing. Toss gently, season with salt, ground pepper and hot pepper flakes. Garnish with finely chopped fresh parsley.

MAMMA'S TIPS

Garnish with cherry tomatoes for added colour and sweetness.

COLD SALTED COD
AND POTATOES

CHEF'S NOTES

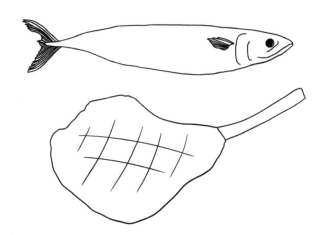

Chapter 8

DESSERT

CANNOLI ALLA SICILIANA

yields: 16 .... time: 2hrs + rest time .... Advanced ....

A Sicilian heirloom dessert that features a flaky and crunchy shell piped full of sweet creamy ricotta filling. Originally the dough was rolled and wrapped around a walking "cane" to hold their shape while frying, hence the name (can'e'oli). Nowadays we recommend metallic tubes to perfect this dreamlike recipe.

EQUIPMENT

Cannoli Tubes

Pasta Machine

Piping Kit

STEP 1 INGREDIENTS

1 cup "00 all-purpose" flour
+ some for kneading

1 Tbsp granulated sugar

1 tsp ground cinnamon or
bitter cocoa

$\frac{1}{4}$ tsp salt

$1\frac{1}{2}$ Tbsp (25 g) pure lard
(or vegetable shortening)

1 egg yolk (reserve egg white for
sealing cannoli shells)

2 tsp white wine vinegar

$\frac{1}{4}$ cup Marsala wine

6 cups (approx.) melted lard or
vegetable oil for deep frying

STEP 1 - CANNOLI SHELLS

DIRECTIONS

Sift together the flour, sugar, cinnamon or cocoa and salt in a bowl.

Cut in the lard, with a fork or hands, until the mixture is grainy. In a small cup, combine egg yolk, wine vinegar and the Marsala wine; stir and add to the flour mixture.

Gather dough and knead for about 5 - 10 minutes on a lightly floured board, until the dough is smooth and springs back when poked.

Shape into a ball, cover and refrigerate for at least 2 hours.

Divide dough into 2 - 3 sections. Work with one section at a time while keeping the unused dough covered. Use a pasta machine to roll out thin strips. Pat dough lightly with flour, run through the first or widest number, several times, folding and reshaping dough, until it is smooth.

Continue running it through, the increasingly finer settings, once only, to about #5 on the pasta machine. You may choose to roll the dough out manually with a rolling pin, on a lightly floured surface, to an evenly thin sheet, about 2 mm thick.

Use a cutter to cut 9 cm circles. Gather scrapped dough and re-use. Repeat until all of the dough is used up.

Wrap each circle around a metal cannoli tube (not too tightly, but not sagging either) and overlap on top; brush under the overlap with egg white, without getting it on the tube, delicately press the edges together and brush more egg white on top to adhere the seam.

In a deep fryer, heat lard or oil to 350°F (180°C). Drop in the cannoli, one or two at a time.

163

STEP 2 INGREDIENTS

1 Kg fresh sheep or best quality whole milk ricotta, strained (amount based on using about 70 g of ricotta per cannolo, and if filling all of the shells at the same time)

1 cup sifted icing sugar

2 tsp vanilla (clear extract or fresh)

½ tsp orange zest

¼ cup candied fruit (optional)

GARNISHING OPTIONS

¼ cup semi-sweet or bitter chocolate shards or chips

¼ cup halved candied cherries

¼ cup crushed pistachios

Shells will bubble up and swell dramatically when frying. Cook until golden and crisp, less than 1 minute.

Remove shells from hot oil carefully, with a slotted utensil or tongs; drain on paper towels. Let cool, then gently slip shells off the tubes (we use pliers). Store shells in an air-tight container, in a cool, dry place (for up to a month).

STEP 2 – CANNOLI FILLING

DIRECTIONS
Strain ricotta of excess water.

In a large bowl, cream by hand or with an electric beater, on low speed, the ricotta, icing sugar, vanilla and zest, just until evenly blended and smooth, 2 minutes.

Fold in your choice of options – chocolate shards and/or candied fruit pieces.

Cover and refrigerate until needed.

When ready to serve cannoli, transfer filling to a pastry bag fitted with a star tip, 2 cm in diameter, and pipe filling into cannoli shells.

Ends may be garnished with either candied cherry, crushed pistachio, chocolate shavings, or kept plain.

Dust shell with icing sugar, if desired.

Serve immediately.

RAVIOLI DOLCI DI CASTAGNE

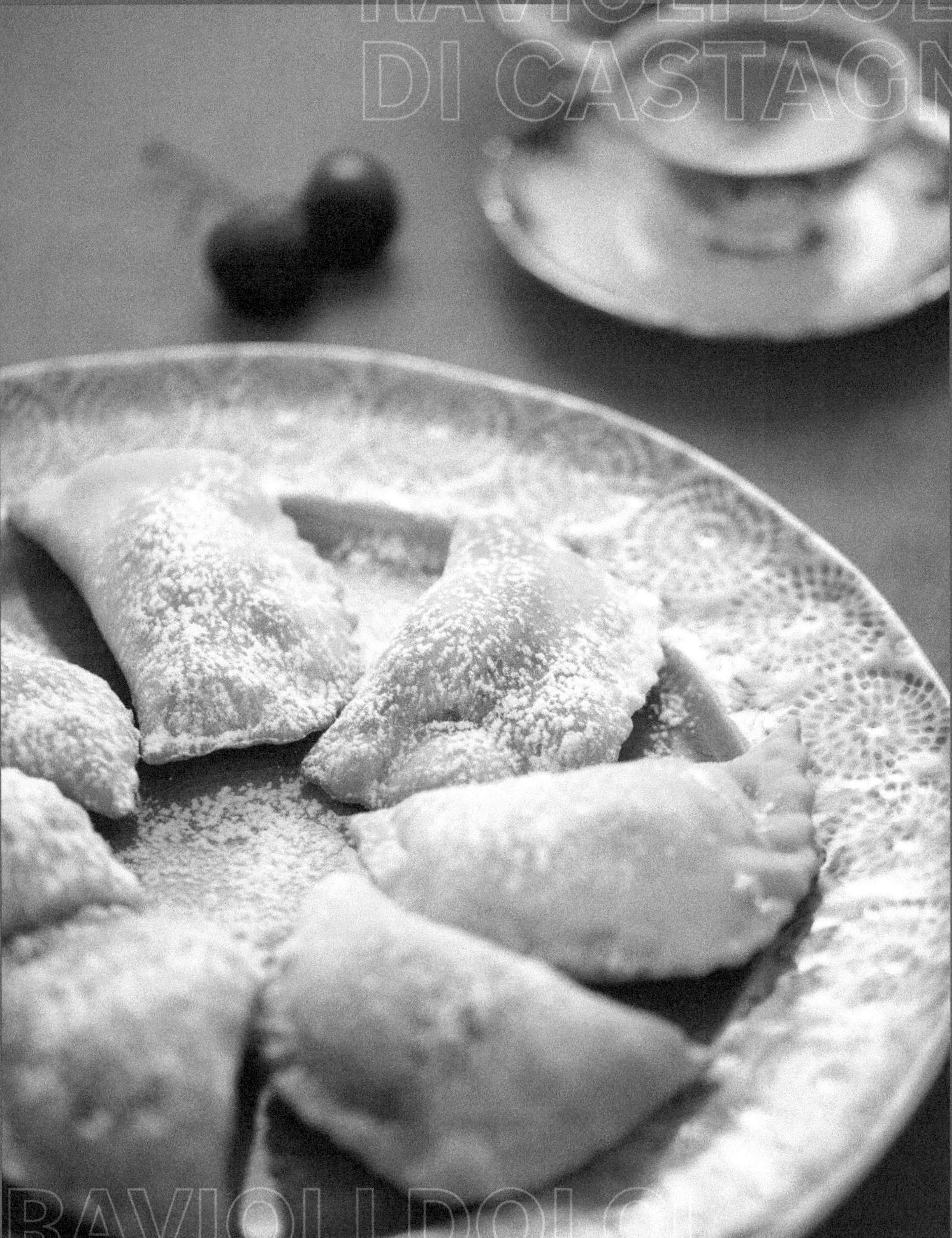

RAVIOLI DOLCI DI CASTAGNE

SWEET CHESTNUT RAVIOLI

yields: 36-40 .... time: 3hrs .... Advanced ....

Sweet dough shaped into half moon pillows, filled with a rich chestnut and chocolate puree, then fried. Usually made at Christmas and Mardi Gras time or whenever chestnuts are in season. A labour of love but so delectably rewarding.

EQUIPMENT

Pasta Machine

Food Mill

Pasta Cutter

STEP 1 INGREDIENTS

500 g chestnuts (with skins)

½ tsp salt

1 bay leaf

½ cup sugar

¼ cup cocoa

¼ tsp ground cinnamon

¼ cup dark rum

¼ cup alchermes or brandy (almond milk also works)

2 Tbsp Nutella (optional)

½ cup sweetened espresso or strong coffee

STEP 2 INGREDIENTS

2 cups (280 g) "00" all purpose flour + more for kneading

¼ tsp salt

2 Tbsp sugar

2 large eggs

2 Tbsp vegetable oil or melted lard

2 Tbsp brandy or rum

2 Tbsp water

½ tsp vanilla

6 cups (approx.) vegetable oil or melted lard for deep frying

STEP 1 – FILLING

DIRECTIONS

Rinse and soak chestnuts in cold water for an hour. Score outer skin on one side (or peel completely). In a heavy pot, cover chestnuts with water. Add salt and bay leaf. Boil and cook for about 30 minutes, until chestnuts are soft. Peel both the outer and inner skins of the chestnuts (for easier peeling, keep unpeeled chestnuts in the hot water). Purée the cooked, peeled chestnuts through a food mill and place in a mixing bowl.

Add sugar, cocoa and cinnamon; combine. Add rum, alchermes (brandy or almond milk) and Nutella. Add the coffee, in gradual amounts, enough to create a mashed potato-like consistency. Blend well.

Cover & refrigerate until ready to use. Can be made a day ahead.

STEP 2 – DOUGH

DIRECTIONS

Combine flour, salt and sugar in a large bowl or on a wooden or marble work area.

In a small bowl, whisk the eggs, oil or melted lard, brandy or rum, water and vanilla together.

Make a well in the center of the flour and pour in the wet ingredients. With a fork, draw in the flour until all is incorporated.

Gather dough into a ball and knead on a floured work area, until no longer sticky, but shiny and smooth, about 10 minutes. Add flour, as needed. Cover and let rest for 30 minutes.

167

STEP 3 – FORMING AND FRYING THE RAVIOLI

DIRECTIONS

Cut one small disc of dough, at a time and leave the rest well-covered. Using a pasta machine, make a fine strip. Progress to #5 or #6 on the machine for the final result.

Place rolled pasta strip on a floured board. Scoop a fully rounded Tbsp of chestnut filling, about 3 cm apart, off-center along the strip. Fold strip over to cover the filling. Stretch & seal dough, cupping each ravioli mound tightly with hands. Using a ravioli cutter, shape into raviolis, crimp around the edges with a fork to seal tightly and set on a well-floured surface; cover with a cloth to prevent from drying, until all are formed.

Deep fry in hot vegetable oil or lard, in batches, turning and keeping them immersed in the oil when they pop up. Remove with a slotted spoon when golden (1 - 2 minutes). Drain on paper towels. Cool, sprinkle with icing sugar and serve.

CROCCANTE DI MANDORLE

yields: approx 20-24 serving pieces .... time: 1hr ....

Croccante is quick to make, easy to store and enjoyed anytime. The rich smell and taste of toasted sugar-coated almonds sets the mood for the holidays and future baking at Christmas time. With just enough sugar to sweeten and coat the almonds, this croccante is softer and easier to cut and enjoy.

INGREDIENTS

4 cups (600g) blanched whole almonds

¼ cup honey

1¾ cup sugar

4 Tbsp water

butter for greasing foil or parchment paper

2 cross-sectioned lemon halves

DIRECTIONS

Preheat the oven to 400°F (200°C) and toast almonds for 8 - 10 minutes. Cool.

Prepare the area for the hot croccante: place a generously buttered sheet of foil or parchment on a board or cookie tray. With one lemon half, squeeze lemon juice over the butter and spread lightly with a brush. Have a few spoons or metal spatulas nearby.

Combine honey, sugar & water in a large, heavy saucepan on medium-high heat. Cook and stir until ingredients liquefy, the sugars turn a rich golden colour and the bubbles start to recede (8 - 10 minutes).

For precision, sugar should reach a temperature of 238°F (114 C°) on a candy thermometer.

Add the almonds; stir continuously until sugar returns to a liquified state and the nuts are well-coated, glazed and caramel coloured (5 - 8 minutes).

When ready, remove immediately from heat and pour or spoon croccante onto the prepared buttered foil or parchment. With the back of a spoon or metal spatula in one hand, and the remaining lemon half in the other, quickly smooth and mold the croccante into the desired shape and uniform thickness.

Let cool completely (30 minutes) before peeling off foil.

Wrap in parchment, then in foil and store in a cool, dark, air-tight container for up to a month.

Cut or break into serving pieces.

MAMMA'S TIPS

Toasted raw (unpeeled) almonds can be substituted.

For added flavour, rub a fresh bay leaf over croccante as it cools.

Mold croccante into any shape – logs, numbers, clusters, wreaths…

AMARETTI

yields: 36-40 .... time: 1hr 30mins + 6-8 hours rest ....

Almond flavoured macaroon-esque cookies that are crunchy on the outside and soft and moist on the inside. Every region of Italy stakes a claim to making the best version of these national treasures, and we too, tout our recipe as best!

EQUIPMENT
Food Processor

Electric Beater

INGREDIENTS
500 g (3½ cups) blanched almonds (or 400 g blanched and 100 g raw or bitter, with skins)

1¾ cups granulated sugar

½ cup (3 - 4) egg whites, at room temperature

¼ tsp cream of tartar

1 Tbsp almond or bitter almond extract

½ cup granulated sugar, for rolling

candied cherries and/or lightly toasted almonds (extra from above), for garnish

DIRECTIONS
On a cookie sheet, roast all of the almonds, in a preheated 400°F (200°C) oven for 8 - 10 minutes or until lightly toasted. Cool. Set aside extra almonds intended for garnish.

Place the measured almonds and sugar together in food processor. Pulse until smooth and evenly ground. Avoid over-grinding as it will draw out too much oil. Place in a mixing bowl and set aside.

Beat egg whites with the cream of tartar and extract, until soft peaks form. Fold the beaten egg whites, a little at a time, into the ground almond and sugar until the mixture is firm, yet sticky enough to bind together. Cover mixture and refrigerate 6 - 8 hours or overnight.

Preheat oven at 325°F (165°C).

Cover two cookie sheets with parchment paper. Place sugar, for rolling, in a mixing bowl.

Halve enough candied cherries or have the extra almonds available for garnish; set aside.

Remove mixture from refrigerator.

Use a small cookie scoop or rounded Tbsp to portion the mixture into balls (about the size of a walnut or golf ball).

Shape into a smooth ball, roll in sugar and place on a parchment-lined cookie sheet, 2 cm apart (cookies will expand slightly in oven).

Hands will get sticky from rolling and may require washing and drying them once or twice during the process. Wearing latex gloves alleviates this problem and makes the task much easier.

Gently press a halved candied cherry or almond on top.

Place cookie sheets in the preheated oven. Bake, 25 - 30 minutes, or until lightly coloured but not browned. Cool on tray.

MAMMA'S TIPS

They freeze well.

Cookies may be kept for several weeks in an airtight container.

ALMOND BISCOTTI

yields: 24 ⸻ time: 1hr ⸻

These classic biscotti, twice baked with a dry, crunchy texture are perfect to enjoy with coffee, wine or as a snack. Biscotti can be stored for weeks in an air-tight container or easily frozen. Get creative and substitute almonds for a variety of other delicious add-ins and make them your personalized favourite biscotti.

INGREDIENTS

1 cup (170 g) whole raw almonds

2½ cups (350 g) all-purpose flour

2 tsp baking powder

½ tsp salt

3 eggs

¾ cup sugar

½ cup melted butter
(or vegetable oil)

zest of ½ lemon

1 Tbsp almond extract

1 beaten egg + 2 Tbsp lemon juice, for brushing on top (optional)

DIRECTIONS

On a cookie sheet, very lightly toast the almonds at 400°F (200°C) for 6 - 8 minutes; cool, roughly chop, each into 3 - 4 pieces and set aside.

Preheat oven to 350°F (180°C). Line a large baking sheet with parchment paper.

In a small bowl, sift and combine flour, baking powder and salt.

In a large bowl, mix, by hand or beat with a hand-mixer, eggs, sugar, melted butter, lemon zest and almond extract, until foamy, 1 - 2 minutes. Stir in the almonds (or add-ins of choice).

Mix or combine other options, such as cranberries, raisins, chocolate chips or other nuts, but keep the quantity at 1 cup.

Add ⅓ of the flour mixture at a time, mixing well, with a spatula, until all is combined.

Gather the sticky dough with the spatula and place onto a floured board. Lightly dust with a sprinkle of flour and pat down with floured hands, kneading gently, until dough is smooth. Divide into 2 logs; arrange on the prepared baking sheet, about 6 cm apart, to allow for expansion, during baking. Smooth the tops and sides and shape into rectangular logs, about 2 - 3 cm thick. Brush logs with egg wash (optional).

Bake until lightly golden, about 25 - 30 minutes. Remove from oven. When cool enough to touch, place one log at a time on the cutting board. With a sharp knife, cut across the log diagonally into finger width slices. (Cut straight down, rather than sawing to avoid crumbs or broken pieces).

Arrange the biscotti, cut side down, on the baking sheet. Re-bake at 350°F (180°C) until pale golden in colour, about 20 more minutes.

Transfer the biscotti to a wire rack and cool completely.

ANISE CANTUCCI

yields: 48 .... time: 1hr ....

Cantucci, the original, fat-free, small and crunchy "biscotti" from Tuscany! Flavoured with either lemon, almond or anise, these delectable nuggets were traditionally served at the end of a meal with a glass of sweet wine, Vin Santo, for dipping. Today, enjoy these easy to make, low-cal gems anytime as a snack, and for dunking.

INGREDIENTS

2 ½ cups all-purpose flour
+ some for dusting

2 tsp baking powder

½ tsp salt

3 eggs

¾ cup granulated sugar

½ cup olive oil

1 Tbsp aniseeds

1 Tbsp liquorice liqueur
(Sambuca, Anisette, Pastis)

DIRECTIONS

Preheat oven to 350°F (180°C). Line a large baking sheet with parchment paper.

In a small bowl, sift and combine flour, baking powder and salt.

In a large bowl, whisk or beat with mixer, eggs and sugar, until foamy, 1 - 2 minutes.

Add the oil, aniseeds and extract. Mix to combine.

Add ⅓ of the flour at a time, mixing well, with a spatula, until all the flour is incorporated. Gather the sticky dough and place on a floured board. Lightly dust dough with a sprinkle of flour and pat down until dough is smooth.

Divide the cookie dough into 4 equal sections (or 3).

Arrange each section into rolls, spaced about 6 cm apart on prepared baking sheet; flatten and shape into smooth rectangular logs, about 2 - 3 cm thick.

Bake until lightly golden, about 20 - 25 minutes. Remove from oven. When cool enough to touch, place one log at a time on the cutting board. With a sharp knife, cut across the log diagonally into finger width slices. (Cut straight down, rather than sawing to avoid crumbs or broken pieces).

Arrange the cantucci, cut side down, on the baking sheet.

Re-bake at 350°F (180°C) until a pale golden colour, another 20 minutes.

Transfer cantucci to a rack and cool completely.

PINEAPPLE COOKIES

yields: 28-30 .... time: 1hr 30mins + rest ....

Pineapple? Italian?... ya, get over it, Sicily is nearly tropical! Sweet purse-like pastry bundles filled with a delightfully refreshing pineapple filling. Light and yummy and difficult to resist.

STEP 1 INGREDIENTS

¼ cup milk, warmed

¼ tsp granulated sugar

1½ tsp (4 g) active dry yeast

1 egg, lightly beaten

¼ tsp salt

½ cup pure lard, room temp.

1½ cups (210 g) all-purpose flour

STEP 2 INGREDIENTS

1 can (540 ml) crushed pineapple, drained

⅓ cup sugar

3 Tbsp (25 g) cornstarch

2 tsp butter

STEP 1 - COOKIE DOUGH

DIRECTIONS

Warm milk, (to the touch, it should be slightly warmer than body temperature). Sprinkle yeast and sugar over the warm milk, gently stir and let rise until doubled in volume, 8 - 10 minutes.

In a medium bowl, combine the beaten egg, salt, and lard, broken down lightly with a spatula. Add the yeast mixture and gently stir.

Add the flour in gradual amounts; with the spatula, blend the flour into the mixture until the flour is integrated and the dough is smooth and sticky. Gather any bits of dough around the bowl and form into a smooth ball, without overworking it (like pie pastry). Cover the bowl with cellophane and refrigerate for 6 hours or overnight.

Prepare the filling.

STEP 2 - PINEAPPLE FILLING

DIRECTIONS

Drain and strain the crushed pineapple, well.

In a saucepan mix the strained, crushed pineapple, cornstarch and sugar.

Cook, over medium heat, stirring regularly, until sugar and starch are dissolved and bubbles break the surface, 3 - 5 minutes. Remove from heat and add butter.

Cover and refrigerate until needed.

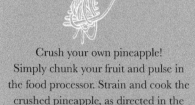

STEF SAYS

Crush your own pineapple! Simply chunk your fruit and pulse in the food processor. Strain and cook the crushed pineapple, as directed in the recipe, and enjoy the leftover juice as a drink.

EQUIPMENT

small rolling pin

parchment-lined cookie sheet

STEP 3 INGREDIENTS

2 cups (approx.) icing sugar

STEP 3 - ASSEMBLY AND BAKING

DIRECTIONS

Preheat oven to 375°F (190°C).

Remove cookie dough from the fridge. For each cookie, take about a tablespoon of dough and form a ball, approximately the size of a large marble.

Place some icing sugar on the work area. With your hand, roll the ball of dough in the icing sugar; with a mini rolling pin, flatten and roll the ball into an even circular disc (roughly the size of a wide jar lid), flipping it over a few times, so that both sides are generously coated with icing sugar.

Fill the center of the disc with a teaspoon of pineapple filling; bring up two sides and gently press and crimp (as with a pie crust), to firmly seal the edges of the seam. Shape into an oval purse-like bundle and set on a prepared cookie sheet. Repeat.

Bake to a delicately coloured crust, in preheated oven, 18 - 20 minutes.

SPINGI DOLCI DI RICOTTA

yields: 18-20 .... time: 1hr ....

The name of these delicious golden puffs varies in different regions of Italy. Whether enjoyed during Carnevale, Easter or Christmas, they are always a hit and quick to make. Delicious, served warm and rolled in sugar and cinnamon!

EQUIPMENT

Deep fryer

INGREDIENTS

1 cup (140 g) all-purpose flour

1½ tsp baking powder

¼ cup granulated sugar

¼ tsp salt

¼ tsp ground cinnamon

2 eggs

1 Tbsp olive oil

1 Tbsp honey

1 tsp vanilla

1 Tbsp rum or brandy

2 Tbsp (30 ml) freshly squeezed orange juice

2 tsp orange zest

1 cup (250 g) ricotta, well drained

2 L vegetable oil for deep-frying

1 cup sugar + ½ tsp cinnamon for rolling

DIRECTIONS

In a small bowl, combine flour, baking powder, sugar, salt and cinnamon; set aside.

In a larger bowl, add the eggs, oil, honey, vanilla, rum, juice and zest; lightly whisk.

Add the ricotta and mix together, to combine.

Stir in the dry ingredients and mix, to a thick, sticky batter. Let stand for 20 minutes or cover and refrigerate for up to 6 hours, until ready to fry.

Heat the oil for deep-frying on medium heat, 350°F(180°C) – 350°F(180°C).

Drop batter, by rounded tablespoonfuls, four or five at a time, into the hot oil. Fry, always on medium heat, flipping over, until spingi are puffed, golden and cooked right through, about 4 minutes in total.

Transfer, with a slotted spoon, to drain on paper towels.

Roll warm spingi, in either plain granulated sugar, a cinnamon and sugar mixture or dust with icing sugar.

CIAMBELLONE AL LIMONE

serves: 12 .... **time: 1hr** ....

A simple, sunshiny Italian tea cake, with a rich crumb and moist spongy centre made in a ring pan with a vanilla-lemon zing to it.

EQUIPMENT
Bundt or Tube Pan

INGREDIENTS

2¼ cups (350 g) all-purpose flour

2 Tbsp (16 g) baking powder

¼ tsp salt

4 eggs

1 cup (200 g) granulated sugar

⅔ cup (150 ml) vegetable oil

zest of 2 lemons

juice of 2 lemons + water to equal ⅔ of a cup

2 tsp vanilla

1 Tbsp sugar, for sprinkling, on top (optional) or finish off after baking

DIRECTIONS
Grease and lightly flour a bundt or tube pan.

Preheat oven to 350°F (180°C).

In a small bowl, combine sifted flour, baking powder and salt.

In a larger bowl, beat eggs and sugar, with a hand mixer, at medium speed, about 2 minutes or until mixture is pale.

Add the oil, zest, lemon juice and vanilla; beat at low speed, just to incorporate.

Add dry ingredients, in gradual amounts. Mix and blend, at low speed or by hand, until batter is smooth.

Spread batter in the prepared pan; sprinkle with sugar or leave plain, to garnish after baking.

Bake at 350°F (180°C) for 40 – 45 minutes or until centre is dry (toothpick test – nothing sticks to toothpick).

Remove from oven and let cake cool in pan for 10 minutes. Loosen edges then remove or invert onto a wire rack.

Serve plain or spruce it up using one of Mamma's tips.

MAMMA'S TIPS

1. Cool and dust with icing sugar before serving

2. Cool and coat with a LEMON GLAZE:
Whisk together 1½ cups icing sugar with
5 - 6 Tbsp lemon juice and
drizzle over cake.

TIRAMISU

serves: 8-10 ·················· time: 1hr 30mins + 6 hours for cooling ·····························

An absolute classic Italian dessert made with stiff beaten egg whites folded into the beaten egg yolk and mascarpone mixture, then layered over espresso-soaked "lady finger" biscuits. A truly joyful pick-me-upper!

EQUIPMENT
Baking Dish

Electric Beater

INGREDIENTS
1½ cups espresso or strong coffee

¼ cup sugar + 2 Tbsp sugar (to sweeten coffee)

½ cup Marsala wine (or rum or brandy), divided

6 eggs, separated, at room temperature

¼ tsp cream of tartar

1 tub (500 g) mascarpone

400 g (about 48) ladyfinger biscuits

¼ cup cocoa powder or shaved semi-sweet chocolate

DIRECTIONS
Make espresso; sweeten with 2 Tbsp sugar and add liqueur; place in a shallow dish that will fit a ladyfinger cookie, for dipping; cool and set aside.

Separate the egg whites and the egg yolks into two mixing bowls. Bring a small saucepan, one quarter filled with water, to a boil, then reduce heat to simmer.

In the bowl with the egg yolks, add ¼ cup of sugar and ¼ cup Marsala, then set the bowl over the saucepan of barely simmering water. With a whisk or a hand-held electric beater, at low speed, whip the egg mixture continuously, until it triples in volume into a thick lemon yellow colour, 8 - 10 minutes. When ready, remove the egg mixture or "sabayon" from the heat; allow to cool slightly before adding the mascarpone. Add the mascarpone and mix until well combined; set aside.

With an electric beater, beat the egg whites with 2 Tbsp sugar and ¼ tsp cream of tartar until stiff peaks form. Fold the beaten egg whites evenly into the egg-mascarpone mixture. Combine evenly.

Have ready a large 33 x 23 x 5 cm (13 x 9 x 2 inch) pyrex pan.

Without soaking, dip one ladyfinger at a time, swiftly on each side, into the coffee mixture; line the bottom of the pan with the dipped ladyfingers.

Spoon half of the mascarpone filling over the lady fingers and spread into an even layer.

Dust half of the cocoa over the filling. Repeat by dipping the remaining ladyfingers into the coffee and arrange a second layer over the filling. Spread the remaining mascarpone mixture over ladyfingers.

Cover the top with the remaining cocoa powder, or shaved chocolate. Cover with plastic wrap and refrigerate for at least 6 hours. Be patient... then enjoy!

MAMMA'S TIPS

For a rich creamier texture, substitute the egg whites for 2 cups (500 ml) whipping cream + 2 Tbsp icing sugar, beaten until stiff peaks form.

CHEF'S NOTES

Chapter 9

BASICS

PASTA DOUGH

serves: 6-8 .... time: 2hrs 30mins .... Advanced ....

Making pasta dough can be enjoyable and therapeutic. However, when you're working with flour and eggs, there are many variables that are difficult to control, so exact measurements can vary. The size of the eggs, the humidity or dryness in the air, or the flour you are using all contribute to how your dough will turn out. Mixing by hand guarantees that you can adjust your dough as you're working. The general rule for measuring flour and egg proportion is 100 g of flour for every egg. The other general premise to go by is one egg will yield two servings. Based on those two generalities, desired quantities can be gauged.

We add extra yolks to our dough to make the dough smooth, malleable and to give it a rich golden colour. As far as flour goes, all-purpose flour works well but we prefer the "00" flour or the double milled durum wheat semolina. The latter has a grainier texture and can be fussier to work with. However, both are of a high grade, refined and specifically milled to achieve a pasta dough that will be silky and maintain its firmness, when cooked.

EQUIPMENT
Pasta Machine

Scraper

INGREDIENTS
3 large eggs + 2 egg yolks

1 Tbsp olive oil

½ tsp salt

2 Tbsp water

3 cups (420 g) "00" flour
+ another cup (approx.)
for kneading

DIRECTIONS
In a small bowl, whisk eggs, oil, salt and water.

Place flour on a board and form a well. It's better to start with a little less flour and add as needed, than to end up with a brittle dough that is hard to knead. Add the egg mixture in the center of the well; with a fork, gradually draw flour from the inner edge of the well, into the center. Continue slowly incorporating until all the flour is used.

Gather dough into a ball and using extra flour, as needed, knead, knead and knead dough until it is no longer sticky, but shiny, smooth and resilient (about 10 minutes). The dough is ready when a finger imprint will rise and negate itself.

Place a few drops of oil on hands, rub onto dough, cover with cellophane and rest for at least 30 minutes in refrigerator, or up to 8 hours. Do not skip this important step.

To stretch dough through a pasta machine: cut a piece of dough, roughly the size of a English muffin (while always keeping the unused dough well covered); flatten and flour on both sides and run it through the first number. If not smooth or even, fold and run through the first number again. Lightly flour dough and continue to run the dough through the subsequent numbers, on the pasta machine, while always keeping dough smooth and floured. The second to last is usually a good final setting, but it varies with each machine.

Set the pasta sheets over a tablecloth or well-floured surface until ready to use.

MAMMA'S TIPS

This egg pasta dough can be used for all types of pasta, including lasagna and cannelloni.

193

VARYING DOUGH PROPORTIONS

Quantity and servings are approximate, rounded off and based on 1 cup of flour weighing 140 g. However, different flours vary in weight.

To make spinach pasta dough, blanch, strain, squeeze-dry and purée spinach, add to the egg mixture and combine, then incorporate into the flour to make the dough. The amount of flour may vary slightly.

For 16 - 18 Servings: 8 eggs + 4 egg yolks, 4 Tbsp olive oil, 1 tsp salt, ½ cup water, 6 cups (840 g) flour plus more for kneading and rolling

For spinach dough: add 450 g fresh spinach, blanched, strained, squeeze-dried and puréed

For 12 - 16 Servings: 6 eggs + 4 egg yolks, 3 Tbsp olive oil, ¾ tsp salt, ⅓ cup water, 5 cups (700 g) flour + more for kneading and rolling

For spinach dough: add 360 g fresh spinach, blanched, strained, squeeze-dried and puréed

For 10 - 12 Servings: (Fills approx. two 28 x 23 x 6 cm pans or one large 36 x 26 x 6 cm pan)
5 eggs + 3 egg yolks, 2½ Tbsp olive oil, ½ tsp salt, ¼ cup water, 4 cups (560 g) flour + more for kneading & rolling

For spinach dough: add 340 g fresh spinach, blanched, strained, squeeze-dried and puréed

For 8 - 10 Servings: (Fills one large roasting/lasagna pan approx. 32 x 23 x 6 cm)
4 eggs + 2 egg yolks, 2 Tbsp olive oil, ½ tsp salt, 3 Tbsp water, 3 cups (420 g) flour + more for kneading & rolling

For spinach dough: add 250 g fresh spinach, blanched, strained, squeeze-dried and puréed

For 6 - 8 Servings: 3 eggs + 2 egg yolks, 1½ Tbsp olive oil, ¼ tsp salt, 2 Tbsp water, 2 ½ cups (350 g) flour + more for kneading & rolling

For spinach dough: add 180 g fresh spinach, blanched, strained, squeeze-dried and puréed

For 4 - 6 Servings: 2 eggs + 1 egg yolk, 1Tbsp olive oil, ¼ tsp salt, 2 Tbsp water, 1½ cups (210 g) flour + more for kneading & rolling

For spinach dough: add 120 g fresh spinach, blanched, strained, squeeze-dried and puréed

FRESH TOMATO SAUCE

serves: 4-6 .... time: 20mins ....

Serve up a delicious plate of pasta with this quick and light tomato sauce. Savour and enjoy the refreshing taste of sweet tomatoes and fresh herb flavours, along with the hot punch of chilli pepper.

INGREDIENTS

¼ cup olive oil

2 cloves garlic, crushed

¼ tsp fresh hot chilli pepper (peperoncino), or to taste

1 Kg (10 - 12) fresh ripe plum tomatoes, skinned, seeded and chopped or crushed

sea salt and freshly ground pepper, to taste

1 tsp each of fresh oregano and parsley, finely chopped

8 - 10 fresh basil leaves, finely chopped or torn

DIRECTIONS

To skin tomatoes, bring a large pot of water to a boil. Score an "X" on the bottom of each tomato and blanch in boiling water for 1- 2 minutes, or until the skin begins to crack. Lift tomatoes with a slotted spoon and place in cold water.

When cool enough to handle; remove skin, gently squeeze water, seeds and white flesh. Chop or crush and set aside.

Heat oil on medium; add and cook garlic and hot chilli flakes until fragrant, 1 - 2 minutes. Add the fresh tomatoes; season with salt, pepper and fresh herbs. Cook sauce just enough for the tomatoes to come to a simmer and lightly thicken (10 - 15 minutes), or as long as it takes for your pasta to cook.

Enjoy the freshness of this "sugo" on your favourite pasta, whenever fresh plum tomatoes are available.

SUGO DI POMODORO

serves: 8-10 ⋯⋯⋯⋯⋯ time: 40mins ⋯⋯⋯⋯⋯⋯⋯

This basic tomato sauce is rich, smooth and more full-bodied than the Fresh Tomato Sauce recipe, on the previous page. It is the go-to sauce when a recipe calls for basic tomato sauce, as in eggplant parmigiana, meatballs, braciole, or for any of the saucy pasta dishes.

INGREDIENTS

¼ cup olive oil

1 large onion, finely chopped

2 cloves garlic, crushed

1 cup white wine

2 L (3 bottles) passata

1½ cups water

2 bay leaves

½ tsp each of salt and freshly ground pepper, or to taste

¼ tsp chilli pepper flakes (optional)

2 Tbsp of combined freshly chopped parsley, basil and oregano or ½ tsp each of dried

DIRECTIONS

Heat oil on medium heat. Add onion and garlic.

Cook until onions are translucent and garlic fragrant (6 - 8 minutes).

Add wine, cook to reduce by half.

Add the passata and water (use the water to rinse the tomato bottles). Add bay leaves and season with salt, pepper, parsley, oregano and/or basil.

Bring sauce to a boil; cook over high heat for 2 - 3 minutes; reduce heat and cook, semi-covered, to a gentle rolling simmer for 20 - 30 minutes or until sauce has thickened enough to coat but not remain on spoon.

RAGU BOLOGNESE

serves: 10-12 .... time: 4hrs ....

A hearty meat sauce – delicious with tagliatelle as per its traditional style in the city of Bologna, but diverse enough to pleasantly complement short pasta, spaghetti or baked lasagna. This is as the tradition goes, so don't be surprised when you see milk in the ingredients.

INGREDIENTS

4 Tbsp olive oil (or half butter and half olive oil)

1 large onion, finely chopped

2 carrots, finely diced

1 celery stalk, finely diced

2 garlic cloves, finely minced

100 g pancetta, finely diced

500 g lean minced beef, fine grind

500 g lean minced pork, fine grind

1 bay leaf

salt and freshly ground pepper, to taste

½ tsp ground nutmeg

1 cup red wine

2 cups whole (full fat) milk, room temperature

2 L (3 bottles) strained tomatoes (passata)

1½ cups water, room temperature

DIRECTIONS

Finely dice onion, carrot and celery, or for a smoother texture, pulse in a food processor, until mixture is broken down into fine pieces.

Heat oil in a heavy saucepan, over medium-high heat and sauté onions, carrots and celery, until softened, 6 - 8 minutes.

Crush garlic and finely chop pancetta, or pulse together in processor, and add to the vegetables; continue cooking another 5 - 8 minutes, or until pancetta is rendered and browned.

Add the minced meat, bit by bit. Stir until evenly browned and no pink remains. Add bay leaf and season with salt, pepper and nutmeg.

Continue cooking another 15 minutes at medium heat.

Raise heat and add wine; simmer until liquid evaporates.

Add the milk; stir and bring to a boil.

Add the tomatoes and water (use water to wash down the tomato bottles). Adjust seasoning. Mix well and return sauce to a boil.

Reduce heat to low and cook partly covered for 2½ - 3 hours, stirring occasionally and adding an extra half to one cup of water, during the cooking time, if sauce appears too thick.

MAMMA'S TIPS

Reduce the amount of tomatoes by half, for a true meaty Bolognese sauce. You can substitute passata for whole canned plum tomatoes.

MEAT SAUCE

serves: 10-12 .... time: 3hrs ....

As an alternative to minced meat, this meat-based tomato sauce is made using various varieties of meats. Once cooked, the sauce-soaked meat is strained from the pot and either served on its own, as a side, or, cleaned and trimmed of fat and bones, cut or shredded into small pieces and returned to the sauce. Smooth or meat-filled, this sauce is rich, robust and very flavourful.

INGREDIENTS

90 ml olive oil (approx.)

750 - 1 Kg beef (chuck or round roast), cut into cubes

500 g pork meat (loin, shoulder), cut into cubes

500 g meat of choice – ribs, sausage

3 garlic cloves, crushed

1 large onion, finely chopped

1 carrot, finely chopped

1½ cup red wine

3 - 800 ml cans crushed tomatoes

3 cups water (about 1 cup of water, per can, for rinsing)

salt and ground pepper to taste

2 bay leaves

¼ tsp. ground nutmeg

¼ tsp ground cloves

freshly chopped or dried, parsley, oregano and basil, to taste

DIRECTIONS

In a large heavy pot, heat oil to medium-high; add the meat, brown well on all sides, then transfer onto a dish.

In the same pan, on medium heat, sauté the garlic, onion and carrots until softened, 5 - 8 minutes.

Raise heat to medium-high, return meat to pot. Add the bay leaves and season with salt, pepper, nutmeg and cloves.

Add the wine, deglaze, scraping off any bits of meat from the pot and cook on high heat, 5 - 8 minutes.

Add the tomatoes; use the water to wash down the tomato cans and add to the pot. Add the remaining herbs – oregano, parsley and basil and stir to combine.

Bring sauce to a boil then reduce heat to medium-low. Simmer, partly covered, for at least 2 hours, until meat is tender, adding extra water if the sauce thickens too much.

Remove from heat. With a slotted spoon, separate the meat from the sauce and discard bay leaves and any meat-fat or bones. Serve the sauce-smothered meat separately, while keeping the sauce smooth, or shred or finely cut the lean parts of the meat and return to the sauce (suitable for lasagna or with polenta).

MAMMA'S TIPS

Enjoy the many options for this sauce.
In particular, the smooth version makes
for a rich and tasty vodka sauce.

BESCIAMELLA

yields: 2 cups ························· time: 15mins ····································

One of the "Mother Sauces" of French cuisine, this white roux has long since been adopted into Italian cuisine. "Besciamell" is a simple combination of flour, butter, milk and nutmeg. It acts as a silky texturizer when added to other foods and is the starting point for many creamy cheesy sauces.

INGREDIENTS

2 Tbsp butter

2 Tbsp all-purpose flour

2 cups warmed whole milk

salt and ground pepper, to taste

a dash of ground nutmeg

DIRECTIONS

Melt butter in a heavy pot over medium heat.

Add flour and cook and whisk until well blended, 2 - 3 minutes.

Add the warmed milk, salt, pepper and nutmeg and cook and whisk everything together. Cook over low to medium heat until sauce is thick and smooth, 10 - 15 minutes.

Cool and place cellophane directly on the surface of the sauce, to prevent a skin from forming. Refrigerate in an air-tight container for up to 5 days.

BRODO

serves: 5-7 litres .... time: 4hrs 30mins ....

A long-simmered homemade brodo, not only soothes the soul but also makes soups, rice, casseroles and other dishes much more flavourful and nutritious. Quantities are flexible and used more as a guide, to suit personal preference. Make your brodo more full-bodied and satisfying by substituting or combining chicken with other poultry pieces such as capon or turkey and by including meat and beef bones. In many regions of Italy, capon broth, particularly when served with cappelletti, is considered to be the ultimate and most desirable.

INGREDIENTS

6 - 8 L (24 - 32 cups) cold water

1 (1½ Kg) raw whole chicken
(or chicken pieces with skin and bone-in)

turkey or capon leg/wing
or quarter

2 - 3 soup bones

500 g beef with bone-in (shanks/ribs)

2 medium onions, peeled and quartered

3 celery stalks with leaves,
cut in half

3 carrots, scrubbed, cut in half

2 ripe plum tomatoes, halved

2 bay leaves

5 - 6 sprigs fresh Italian parsley

½ tsp whole peppercorns

2 Tbsp salt or to taste

DIRECTIONS

Place all ingredients in a large heavy pot and fill with cold water. On high heat, cover with lid and bring to a boiling point. Reduce to medium-high and cook at a gentle roll for 20 - 30 minutes, skimming away any scum with a slotted spoon or skimmer.

Reduce heat to medium-low for a rolling simmer and cook, covered, for about 4 hours.

To keep the chicken-meat from overcooking in the broth, remove it after 2 hours. Carefully transfer chicken onto a large dish; when cool enough to handle, remove the perfectly poached meat and return the skin and bones back in the broth. Cut, shred and reserve chicken pieces for other uses (soups, salads, fillings etc.).

After 4 hours of simmering, turn off heat and cool uncovered, on stove. Discard vegetables, bones, skins and seasonings.

Strain broth through a cheesecloth, so that it is clear and amber in colour.

Store extra broth, in an airtight container, in refrigerator, for up to a week or freeze in small containers.

MAMMA'S TIPS

For fat-free broth, refrigerate overnight, then skim fat from the surface. Broth can also be made with the bones, skin and carcass of an already roasted bird, after the meat has been removed.

CHEF'S NOTES

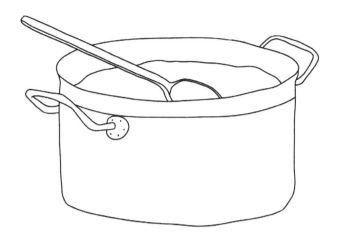

PANTRY

The proceeding pages provide a visual index of all the ingredients we have in our pantry and use in our recipes.

Some are shown in their pure, raw forms, so may look different upon purchase depending on where the grocery shopping is done.

Buying fresh is always best, but many of the recipes cater very well to canned, jarred, shelled, trimmed, ground, peeled, frozen, packaged, bagged, or dried versions of the same.

As always, in the kitchen, there is room for improvisation and substitution to cater to what you have at your disposal, what is convenient, what is freshest, or what is the best value. You be you.

ELABORATIONS

FRESH PASTA

Many recipes involve more than one step. Plan ahead and stagger the steps from one day to the next. In our selection of recipes, fresh pasta is used to make lasagna strips, cappelletti and agnolotti.

CAPPELLETTI VS. TORTELLINI

Cappelletti and tortellini are very similar. Cappelletti look like little hats whereas tortellini are said to represent "Venus's belly buttons". One starts off with a square shape while the other is made from a round shape. When made small, they are usually served in broth, as a soup. Regardless of shape or term, they are interchangeable.

AGNOLOTTI VS. RAVIOLI

For all intents and purposes, there is no difference between the two terms. They are both filled pastas and larger than cappelletti or tortellini. Agnolotti got its name from the Piedmont region of Italy. Today, the names are interchangeable, filled with a variety of stuffings and shaped either square, half-moon or round. The filling can be placed between two layers of dough and cut all around or on one sheet of dough, folded over and cut as a half-moon. Agnolotti or ravioli are usually gently boiled and then served with a sauce.

TYPES OF PASTA

In our recipes, we have recommended dry, packaged pastas that pair well with the suggested sauces, but it's true... some are tough to find, tough to eat, or just less appealing to some tastes. So, pick a different pasta and use it in place of the one we recommend... go on you little rebel, deviate!

In terms of substitutions, short noodles swapped for short noodles and long noodles swapped for long noodles is a good rule of thumb... but heck, you only live once, break the rules and cook the pasta of your pleasure with the sauce that calls your name.

PASTA

Strozzapreti

Fusilli

Penne

Linguine

Bucatini

Zitoni

Mezzi Rigatoni

Spaghetti

Conchiglie or Abissine Rigate (Shells)

EGGPLANT

Eggplant (Aubergine, Melanzana) is classified as a fruit but used as a vegetable and comes in many shapes and sizes. It is meaty, spongy and absorbent and used in such dishes as Eggplant Parmigiana, Caponata and in a variety of other dishes.

Two basic types are interchangeably used in Italian cooking.

The most common and readily available eggplant is glossy, dark purple, oval in shape, rather thick-skinned and spongy, and, if not prepared properly, somewhat on the bitter side. Salting and sweating allows the eggplant to release its bitter juices and make it less absorbent when cooking. The eggplant is sliced or cubed, salted, weighed down in a strainer and allowed to sweat for 30 minutes or longer. It's then rinsed and dried and used according to the recipe.

The Sicilian eggplant, although not as readily available, is more refined and sought after. It is plump and round with a lighter purple and more tender skin. It has a firm, dense, almost seedless flesh, very sweet and not bitter. For that reason, it is not necessary to sweat it before using it.

MUSHROOMS

Because mushrooms are porous and absorb a lot of moisture, they should not be washed. To clean, simply wipe them with a cloth or paper towels, scraping off dirt or debris. Store in a paper bag to avoid moisture condensation. Mushrooms can be substituted for one another in all of our recipes, though the recommended variety will be best.

PORCINI (CÉPES, BOLETE) SHELF LIFE: 2 DAYS

Brown-capped with a thick white stem, porcini mushrooms are widely used in Italy and France with a limited seasonal window. Because of their scarcity in other regions, porcini can be bought as dried mushrooms, hydrated by soaking in warm water, then rinsed and strained, reserving the strained water to be used as a liquid or broth when preparing a dish. Dried mushrooms need only to be used sparingly as they have a strong flavour.

BUTTON (WHITE)

Mild, soft, white.

CREMINI (BROWN, BABY BELLA)
Mild-flavoured with a typical mushroom texture and goes well with everything.

TRUMPET MUSHROOMS (FRENCH HORN, BABY OYSTER)
Velvety-soft in texture with a buttery sweet flavour, great for grilling or for sauces, a great all-round mushroom.

TOMATOES
Tomatoes come in many varieties and although classified as a fruit, they are consumed as a vegetable. They can be enjoyed raw, cooked in different ways, used for sauces or processed for tomato based products. Italian cuisine relies heavily on fresh, canned or bottled tomatoes and tomato paste.

Italian style plum (Roma, San Marzano) tomatoes are renowned as being the best for cooking. San Marzano, is the name of the town in Italy, where, because of the ideal climate and soil conditions, these exceptionally flavourful tomatoes are grown. They are red, firm, egg-shaped, fleshy tomatoes with fewer seeds and very low water content, making them meaty and perfect for tomato sauce.

Fresh vine-ripened tomatoes make exceptional sauce but the next best option is to use good quality canned or processed tomatoes, be it passata (bottled tomato puree), whole plum, crushed or diced.

ARTICHOKES
Globe artichokes belong to the thistle family of plants. Artichokes grow abundantly in southern Italy, as well as in other parts of the world. They are prepared in many different ways: stewed, stuffed, fried, used in salads, with pastas, meats, in risottos or in fillings. When buying artichokes look for ones that are firm, closed, have a long stem and are not bruised.

Canned artichoke hearts, either whole or quartered can be used for fillings and also work well as part of an appetizer tray. For some recipes, (Stuffed Artichokes) there are no exceptions for fresh whole artichokes.

VEGETABLES

Tomatoes

Onions (White, Yellow, Red)

Carrot

Shallots

Spring Onion (Green Onion)

Garlic

Bell Peppers

Spinach

Celery

Artichoke

Cremini Mushroom

White Button Mushroom

Eggplant

Porcini Mushroom

Zucchini

Sicilian Eggplant

Fennel

Potatoes

Butternut Squash

Black Olives (pitted)

Green Olives

Capers

FRUIT

Pineapple

Oranges

Lemons

Raisins

Pears

Red Candied Cherries

Green Candied Cherries

Apples

CURED PORK CUTS

GUANCIALE

Also called pork jowl or pork cheek, this cut of meat resembles bacon in that it's fatty, often gets served thinly sliced, and a little bit goes a long way. It's a rich, fatty piece of meat that often gets cured before it's used. Guanciale devotees claim there is no substitute for it. It's not very easily found in the United States for several reasons, one of which is that the FDA has banned all imports of this meat from Europe. Luckily, Canadian and American farmers are catching on to this succulent fat, ideal for cooking. The fat lends marvelous flavor to any meal, most especially pasta dishes.

PANCETTA

Pancetta comes from the belly of the pig that has been cured in salt, spices and various herbs. It is usually cut into very thin slices and popular in many pasta dishes or sauces. Pancetta is indeed more similar to bacon than to guanciale, but even bacon and pancetta are cured and cut differently, characteristics which distinguish them from one another.

BACON

Bacon can come from several areas of the pig. Lean cuts are from the back, while meatier cuts are taken from the side of the pig or the belly. Belly meat is streaked with fat, and when it's fried it curls up and turns delectably crispy. It's usually cold smoked, which means it's still raw after the process.

PROSCIUTTO

Prosciutto is an Italian dry-cured ham that is usually thinly sliced and served uncooked; this style is called prosciutto crudo in Italian and is distinguished from cooked ham, prosciutto cotto.

MEAT

Chicken Breast

Ribs (Pork Back)

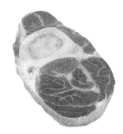

Veal Shank

Pork Tenderloin

Turkey Wings

Beef Chuck

Center Loin (Pork)

MEAT & EGG

Italian Sausage (Pork)

Egg

Mortadella

Prosciutto

Ham (Black Forest)

Guanciale (Pork Jowl)

Pancetta

Bacon

SEAFOOD

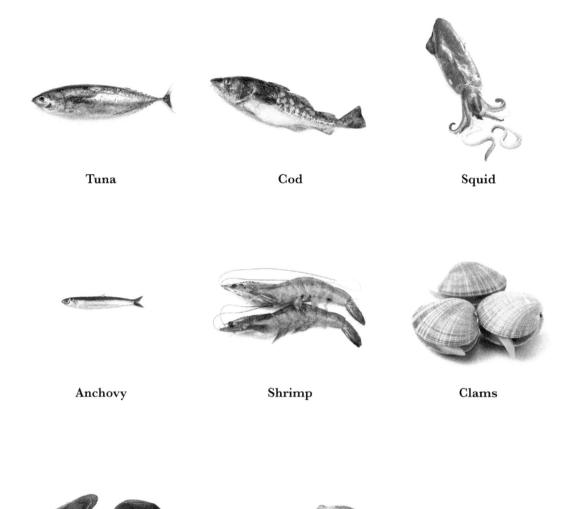

Tuna

Cod

Squid

Anchovy

Shrimp

Clams

Mussels

Scallops

ARBORIO / CARNAROLI / VIALONE NANO RICE

The three popular types of rice for making a great risotto are arborio, carnaroli, and vialone nano.

They all make a fine risotto and differ mainly in grain size and starch content.

The higher the starch content, the creamier the risotto. For that reason, rice should not be rinsed when making risotto.

ARBORIO

The most widely available. This medium-grain rice makes a fine risotto; however, because it is not as starchy as the others, it can overcook more easily and become mushy.

CARNAROLI

Considered the "king" of risotto rices and makes the creamiest risotto. Because of its longer grains and higher starch content, it has a firmer texture and is more forgiving to cook with.

VIALE NANO

A shorter grain rice, grown in northern Italy. It too has a high starch content and makes a creamy risotto, but cooks up more quickly than carnaroli.

BREAD & GRAINS

Polenta

Bread Crumbs
(and Panko Crumbs)

Barley

White Bread

Baguette

Lady Finger Biscuits

Rice (Arborio)

Semolina

PARMESAN VS. PECORINO

Both parmesan and pecorino are hard cheeses and made using the same method.

Parmesan is made from cow's milk while pecorino is made from sheep's milk; the difference in taste is based on the ageing time, and the flavour of the milk.

In Italian cooking, both are grated and added to dishes or shaved and used as a garnish.

Both taste best when bought in a large chunk and grated as needed.

Parmigiano Reggiano, from Parma, in northern Italy is considered superior to the others.

Pecorino is one of the most popular Italian cheeses, with every region claiming its own very best.

BOCCONCINI VS. MOZZARELLA

Bocconcini or baby fresh mozzarella balls are soft, mild unripened cheese made either from cow or buffalo milk. Drained, sliced, bocconcini are great in salads, on pizza, or served as appetizer bites.

Mozzarella is a smooth fresh white cheese made from cow or buffalo milk with a mild sweet flavour. It melts well and is great on pizzas, lasagna or casserole dishes.

RICOTTA VS. RICOTTA SALATA

Ricotta is traditionally made from the whey leftover from other cheeses. Fresh ricotta is semi-ripened cheese made from sheep or whole milk. It is sweet, soft and creamy and can be eaten with a spoon. Ricotta is used extensively in Italian baking and cooking. "Ricotta" means re-cooked while "salata" means salted.

Ricotta salata is a Sicilian delicacy. It is ricotta that has been salted, aged, dried and often double-baked, making it firm enough to grate, shred or to eat as a semi-soft cheese.

CHEESE

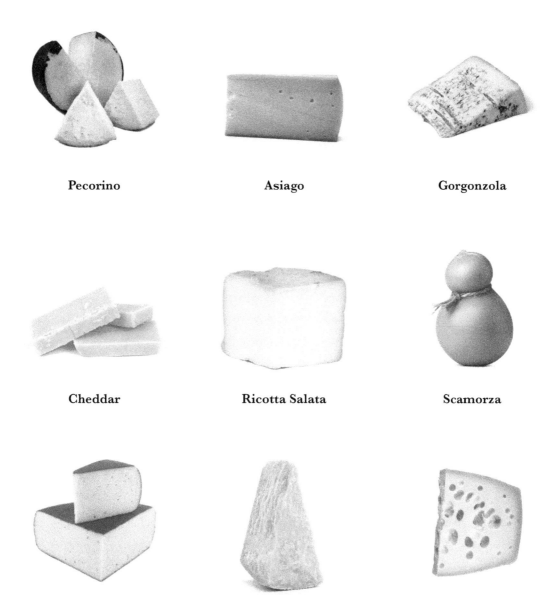

Pecorino

Asiago

Gorgonzola

Cheddar

Ricotta Salata

Scamorza

Fontina

Parmesan (Parmigiano)

Gruyere

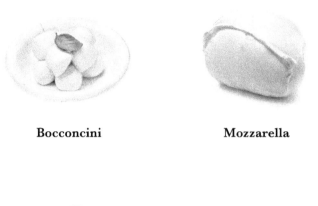

Bocconcini

Mozzarella

Swiss

Mascarpone

Ricotta (fresh)

Goat Cheese

NUTS

Almonds

Pistachios

Chestnuts

Walnuts

Pine nuts

HERBS

Basil

Parsley

Mint

Oregano

Bay Leaves

Rosemary

Thyme

Marjoram

Sage

SAFFRON

Middle Eastern in origin, saffron is the most expensive spice by weight, mainly because of the labour-intensive process required in extracting the stigma of the crocus flower, from which it derives. Although only a small amount of the vivid crimson threads are required to impart flavour and colour to a dish, its quality and hue are determined by its origin. Usually sold as threads or in powdered form, threads being more pure and authentic.

NUTMEG

Nutmeg is derived from a native Indonesian tropical evergreen tree, Myristica fragrans, which produces two spices: nutmeg from the inner seed, and mace from the substance that covers the seed. The nutmeg seeds are dried gradually in the sun until the nutmeg shrinks away from its hard seed coat. When the seed kernels rattle in their covering, the seeds are removed from its outer coat (the mace), and sold whole or ground.

Nutmeg has a long culinary history and can be part of both sweet and savory dishes. It is used in stuffings, sauces, meat dishes and also in baking. It has a distinctive nutty, earthy, slightly sweet yet intense and distinct taste.

Whole nutmeg is grayish-brown and egg-shaped, approximately the size of an apricot pit.

Grating the seed directly into a recipe will impart a fresher, cleaner taste than using store-bought ground nutmeg.

PEPERONCINO

The generic Italian name for hot chilli peppers. Whether fresh or dried red flakes, these hot peppers contain a lot of heat and are therefore used sparingly or according to palatable preferences.

In Italy, the term peperoncini (plural of peperoncino) refers to the many hot varieties of chilli peppers. Dried red chilli pepper flakes are made from a variety of chilli peppers.

Peperoncino adds spice, flavor, heat and punch to many recipes. For spicy food lovers, peperoncino becomes almost addictive, and will be added to virtually everything – fish, vegetables, pasta, sauces, soups, stews, and egg dishes.

Hot peppers are preserved in oil to produce flavorful, spicy oil.

SPICES

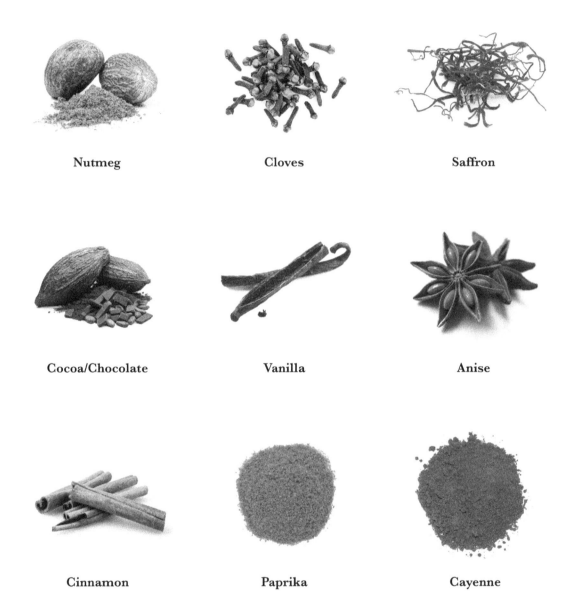

Nutmeg	Cloves	Saffron
Cocoa/Chocolate	Vanilla	Anise
Cinnamon	Paprika	Cayenne

Turmeric   Ginger   Mustard Seed

Chilli flakes (Peperoncino)   Salt and Pepper

POWDERS

Flour (all purpose, '00)

Sugar (granulated)

Cream of Tartar

Yeast

Icing Sugar

Baking Powder

Cornstarch

MARSALA

A fortified wine from Marsala, Sicily, that comes in many degrees of dryness and sweetness. Used in cooking, such as in Veal Marsala, as well as in many desserts (Tiramisu, Sweet Chestnut Ravioli filling...)

OLIVE OIL VS. VEGETABLE OIL

Olive oil is a natural juice that is extracted from only pressed olives. It has a distinct taste that can add flavor and aroma to foods, like pastas or grilled vegetables.

Because of its lower fat content, olive oil has a lower smoke point than vegetable oil so it is best used for enhancing flavour in a dish cooked in moderate-high heat or used raw as in salads or for drizzling over an already cooked dish.

In contrast, vegetable oil is made by mixing oils from different sources, such as canola, cottonseed, sunflower, soybean, corn, and safflower.

Vegetable oil also has virtually no taste and will not impact the overall flavor of a dish when baking or cooking foods.

Vegetable oil has a higher smoke point than olive oil, making it a better option when cooking at extremely high temperatures, such as frying.

BALSAMIC VINEGAR

Balsamic vinegar is sweet, dark, flavourful and concentrated vinegar originating in Modena, Italy.

There are many standards and quality-levels based on the aging process of balsamic vinegar, and as such, its price and uses vary significantly. It is used in salad dressings, in marinades or for syrup reductions, to drizzle over foods and desserts.

OIL, VINEGARS & ALCOHOL

Olive Oil

Balsamic Vinegar

Red Wine Vinegar

White Wine Vinegar

Red Wine

White Wine

Marsala Wine

Alchermes Liqueur

Rum (Dark)

Brandy

Vodka

LIQUIDS & SPREADS

Lard

Coffee

Butter

Heavy Cream

Dijon Mustard

Honey

Maple Syrup

Milk

EQUIPMENT AND UTENSILS

A comprehensive list of equipment you'll need to master all of the classics. There is room for improvisation or alternate tools to do the same job, but these are the ones we're accustomed to using. We've gone electric with our pasta machine, but spent years doing it with the hand crank.

Meat Grinder

Food Scale

Pasta Machine

Mortar and Pestle

Food Processor

Pasta Strainer

Food Mill / Potato Ricer

Dutch Oven

Electric Beater

Dough Scraper

Cheese Grater

Zester / MicroPlaner

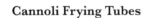

Citrus Juicer

**Pasta Cutters / Fluted
Dough Wheel**

Gnocchi Board

Cannoli Frying Tubes

Nut Cracker

Slotted/Skimming Spoon

Garlic Press

Candy Thermometer

Peeler

Kitchen Shears

Bundt Pan

Large Pot and Steamer

Knife Set (Chef, Bread, Carving, Utility, Paring)

Frying Pan

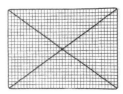

Wire Rack

Meat Tenderizer

Wooden Spoons

Oven Mitt

Cutting Board

Apple Corer

GLOSSARY OF TERMS

Source: *University of Toronto / Food Services*

https://ueat.utoronto.ca – Kitchen Basics Techniques

AL DENTE
To cook food until just firm, just shy of cooked usually referring to pasta or vegetables

BAKE
To cook food in an oven using dry heat

BASTE
To moisten food while cooking by spooning, brushing, or squirting a liquid to add flavour and prevent food from drying out

BEAT
To stir rapidly in a circular motion using a whisk, spoon, or mixer

BRAISE
To cook first by browning in butter or oil, then gently simmering in a small amount of liquid over low heat for a long period of time in a covered pan until tender

BROIL
To expose food to direct heat on a rack or spit, often to melt, brown or toast food like cheese

BROWN
To cook over high heat (usually on the stove-top) to brown food

CARAMELIZE
To heat sugar until it liquefies and becomes a syrup

CHOP
To cut vegetables into large squares, usually specified by the recipe

CREAM
To beat ingredients (usually sugar and a fat) until smooth and fluffy

CUBE
Like chopping, it is to cut food into small cubes

DICE
To cut into very small pieces

DOLLOP
A spoonful of semi-solid food (whipped cream or mashed potatoes), placed on top of another food

DREDGE
To lightly coat uncooked food with flour, cornmeal, bread crumbs or other dry mixture before frying or sautéing

DRESS
To coat foods with a sauce, such as salad

DRIZZLE
To pour liquid, in a stream, back and forth over a dish (melted butter, chocolate, oil or syrup

DUST
To coat lightly with powdered ingredients such as icing sugar, cocoa etc.

FILLET
To cut the bones from a piece of meat, poultry, or fish

FOLD
To combine light ingredients, such as whipped cream or beaten eggs whites, with a heavier mixture, using an over-and-under motion

GLAZE
To coat foods with mixtures such as jellies or sauces

GRATE
Grinding or creating tiny pieces of food, like cheese, for use in a sauce or over food

GREASE
To coat the inside of a pan or dish with shortening, oil or butter to prevent sticking during cooking or baking

JULIENNE
Cutting vegetables into long, thin strips

KNEAD
The process of mixing dough with hands or a mixer

MARINATE
To soak meat, poultry or fish in sauce or flavoured liquid for period of time

MINCE
To cut as small as possible, most commonly used with garlic

PAN FRY
Cook larger chunks of food over medium-heat, flipping once only

PARBOIL
To partially cook, by boiling, usually to prepare food for cooking by another method

POACH
To cook over very low heat, in barely simmering water just to cover

PURÉE
To mash or grind food until completely smooth

ROAST
Like baking but concerning meat or poultry

SAUTÉ
To cook small pieces of food with oil, over a medium-high heat; to brown food

SEAR

To brown the surface of meat by quick-cooking over high heat, to seal in the meat's juices

SHRED

Using a grater with larger holes to form long, smooth stripes of vegetables, cheeses etc.

SIMMER

Bring a pot to a boil, then reduce the heat until there are no bubbles

SKIM

To remove fat or foam from the surface a liquid (e.g. making broth)

SLICE

To cut vertically down, thickness sometimes specified by the recipe

STEAM

To cook food on a rack or in a steamer set over boiling or simmering water

STEEP

To soak a dry ingredient in a very hot liquid (just under the boiling point) flavour, such as with tea or dried mushrooms

STEW

To cook covered over low heat in a liquid for a long period of time

WHIP

To beat food with a whisk or mixer to incorporate air and increase volume

WHISK

To beat ingredients with a fork or a whisk

ZEST

The outer, coloured peel of a citrus fruit

DASH & ZEST

1/8 teaspoon & 1/16 teaspoon, respectively

INDEX

Conversion Charts (most conversions are rounded off to their nearest equivalency, for easy calculation)

ABBREVIATIONS

F	fahrenheit
C	celsius
Kg	kilo
lb	pounds
g	gram
L	liter
oz	ounce
Tbsp	tablespoon
tsp	teaspoon
c	cup

FAHRENHEIT TO CELSIUS

32 °F	0 °C
200 °F	90 °C (warming oven temperature)
225 °F	110 °C
300 °F	150 °C
325 °F	165 °C
350 °F	180 °C (moderate oven temperature)
375 °F	190 °C
400 °F	200 °C (hot oven temperature)
425 °F	220 °C
450 °F	230 °C
500 °F	260 °C (very hot / broiling temperature)

LINEAR REFERENCES

2.5 cm = 1 inch

PAN SIZES

Tube or bundt pan: 23 cm = 9 inches
                              25 cm = 10 inches

Rectangular pans: 33 x 23 cm = 13 x 9 inches
                              28 x 18 cm = 11 x 7 inches

Deep baking dishes: 36 x 26 x 6 cm = 14 x 10 x 2 ½ inches
                              32 x 23 x 6 cm = 12 x 9 x 2 ½ inches
                              28 x 23 x 6 cm = 11 x 9 x 2 ½ inches

Large cookie sheets: 27 x 39 x 2 cm = 10 x 15 x 1 inches
                              32 x 44 x 5 cm = 12 x 17 x 1 inches

WEIGHT REFERENCES

1 Kg = 2.2 (2) lbs
454 (500) g = 1 lb = 16 oz
30 g = 1 oz

BUTTER

1 cup = 230 ml = 16 Tbsp = 8 oz = 2 sticks
½ cup = 115 ml = 8 Tbsp = 4 oz = 1 stick

FLOUR

1 cup all-purpose flour = 140 g = 16 Tbsp = 4 ½ - 5 oz

SUGAR

1 cup granulated sugar = 210 g = 16 Tbsp = 7 oz
1 cup powdered (confectioner's) sugar = 130 g = 16 Tbsp = 4 ½ - 5 oz

BASIC CONVERSIONS AND EQUIVALENTS

Dry Measurements (weight):

1 cup = 240 g = 16 Tbsp = 8 oz

1 tsp = 5 g

1 Tbsp = 15 g

Liquid Measurements (volume:)

1 cup = 240 (250) ml = 8 fl oz

2 cups = 500 ml = 1 pint

4 cups = 1 L (34 fl oz) = 1 quart = 32 oz

Jarred or bottled tomatoes: 800 ml = 28 oz = 3 cups approx

MISCELLANEOUS

1 slice soft bread = ½ cup soft crumbs

1 cup shredded mozzarella = 100 g = approx 4 oz

2 packed cups fresh greens (basil, spinach, arugula) = approx 110 g = 4 oz

60 g prosciutto or pancetta = 2 oz

ACKNOWLEDGEMENTS

We put months of hands-on work into bringing this cookbook to fruition, but we were not by any means, the sole contributors to making it a reality. There are many wonderful people who made big contributions, and they deserve a shout out.

Dominic – Mamma's husband, Stef's dad, felt the brunt of our spinning wheels. While Mamma and Stef tore the kitchen apart cooking, Dom was usually "barked at'" to take care of anything and everything else that needed doing, or to help with shopping, photography, cleaning up, or tasting with expectation for refined opinion. He was the first set of eyes over most of the recipes, designs, and stories and was asked for his two cents' worth on just about every decision we made. Dom also took a major role once we moved to the publishing process, wheeling and dealing, learning the industry, and liaising multiple avenues to ensure we had a quality product that was deliverable around the world. Thanks Mimmo.

Jay, Jazz, Mila, Layla – Son and Brother to Mamma and Stef respectively. Jay and his family of ladies were of great help in facilitating Stef's homecoming and his ability to work with Mamma. Whether it be chauffeuring, photography, tasting opinion or recreating recipes to test on their own, Jay and family were eager to help. The two young girls Mila and Layla qualify as some of our toughest critics and keep us in line for ensured quality control.

Mandy and Lisa – Daughter and Sister to Mamma and Stef respectively. Mandy and her partner Lisa have been very helpful from over many seas, in Australia, in testing recipes, style consultations, and extended networking to get all our ducks in a row.

Flory, Rachel, Lucy, Nadia, Elisa, Marianne, Joanne, Mary – Family recipe testers: these are some of the amazing ladies in the family, who, with their own knowledge and background experience, were most helpful in testing out our family dishes. Their cooperation and support went a very long way in validating the legitimacy of the recipes. Being able to include them in the project helped to realize the potential for family cooking using our recipes.

Maria Gagliardi – has been a long time friend of the family and has been our preferred photographer for everything from weddings to family portraits. She's also well accomplished in food photography and shot and edited our promo video featuring the lasagna recipe. Maria should be called upon for any of your photography needs. Check her @marypics or @blackrammedia

Drew Williams – is a cousin of ours that Stef re-united with on an unexpected layover in Paris. Drew is a digital publisher, and when we touched base with him, he had all sorts of advice and offered help and assistance to every end. He eventually and inadvertently led us to our photographers and designers, double checked almost everything and ensured our Map of Inspiration was able to inspire. Check his work at @swaggermagazine

Molly Young – I reached out to Molly's other half to test a recipe for me, which he did with pleasure, and she replied offering her expertise in the way of proofreading. We of course took her up on it and couldn't be happier with the thorough job she did for us. We took her up on a prompt for further advice, and although she had a full plate at the time, she tagged in her mother Suzy, and she polished up a good part of our story.

Leigh Tynan – Leigh took our photography, our ideas and our expertise to the next level as she stepped in and took the big shots that you see on the cover and the chapter spread pages. With loads of experience at her Toronto Studio "Tynan Studios" she is well versed in all things photography and turned our photo shoot into an array of masterpieces with her food stylings, assisted lighting, and creative touch into every shot.

Mish and Ben Phillips – An old teammate and friend in the world of Ultimate frisbee, Mish and her brother Ben facilitated our self-publishing process from their Melbourne based Hambone Publishing. Ironically enough, they got into the business by publishing a book for their own mother, and it was all too perfect to be able to work with them after having an established relationship, and keeping theme with maternal co-working. They worked well together, and were very responsive to our every need. Go check out Hambone Publishing.

Raquel Buchbinder – As recommended by Leigh Tynan, Raquel is a typesetting and design specialist that Leigh worked wonders with in the past. After shooting with Leigh, Raquel's name came up on multiple occasions, and it seemed like the only way to move forward. Her design work set the tone for the typesetting Hambone Publishing used as guidelines, and her cover art is a thing of beauty that we're proud to adorn our book with.

Dopo il pesce, mangia noci; dopo la carne, cacio.

After eating fish, serve nuts; after meat, cheese.

– An old proverb that Mamma's Uncle Mimmo lived by

RECIPE TESTERS

We are very lucky to have a network of friends and family that have been so gracious to help.

Although these recipes are tried, tested, and true, they have only been so diligently tested by the same eyes over the years. It was time to re-create all of our recipes personally, but we wanted to improve our quality for output by having our peers recreate our recipes in order to ensure that the ingredients were attainable, instructions understandable, and final products looked, smelled and tasted the same as what we were promoting.

We learned heaps from the process, and it helped to create many modifications, and deviations alike to ensure the book was consumable to all and any who wished to try.

Our recipe testers come from all walks of life, with a flair for food as a binding quality we sought before reaching out.

A big thanks to the following:

Joanne Alfonsi
Marianne Alfonsi
Joey Anchondo
Rose Aplidgiotis
Mimi Attardo
Pina Attardo
Remi Bun
David Buzzelli
Earl Cahill
Nikki Collum
Timocles Copland
David Dawson
Ian Dawson

Lisa Deller
Terry Dewar (photo provided – Ciambellone)
Gina Dilanni
Julie DiPietro
Toni Fede
Maria Gagliardi
Lina Ippolito
Mary Kelly
Jazz Konopek
Claire Lavin
Fran Maggio
Lucy Mendola
Nadia Mendola
Justin Orrell
James Price (photo provided – Artichoke Agnolotti)
Amanda Rappazzo
Jay Rappazzo
Enrique Romeiro
Angela Santarelli
Giovanni Santucci
Rita Savatteri
Elisa Scorniaenchi
Jack Sondag
Aaryn Stansell
Anna Piccoli
Jacqueline Tanzella (photo provided - Anise Cantucci)
Flory Zanini
Rachel Zanini

ABOUT THE AUTHORS

STEFAN RAPPAZZO

Over the past 20 years of living abroad and relocating between continents and countries, Stefan had always pursued his passion for food and eventually ditched his decade-long teaching career to embark upon entrepreneurial culinary endeavours and embrace his passion.

Born in Canada, with Italian blood, he decided to take Mamma's recipes on the road.

Stefan made food his full-time interest when he left a teaching career to sling Italian Sandwiches (Pazzo Panini) out of a van in Australia. With an unquenchable thirst for adventure, Stefan sold the business and jumped on an opportunity to own and operate a restaurant in a northern Nicaragua surf-town. "Pasta La Vista", as it came to be known, was a smashing success treating locals and tourists alike to some delectable eats, and wild party nights until the national crisis in 2018 debilitated tourism and as such forced a shutdown and another continental move to Europe. Both the food truck in Australia and the restaurant in Nicaragua featured many of the recipes passed on from his mamma which are included in these pages.

stefpazzo.com

MARY-LOUISE RAPPAZZO

"We are what we eat"...

For Mary-Louise, the art of food preparation is an integral part of who she is. It invokes love, joy, togetherness, cultural identity, tradition, family and personal satisfaction.

Mary-Louise was born in Ascoli Piceno, in Le Marche, Italy and immigrated to Hamilton, Ontario Canada, with her parents, at the age of 6. Educated in Hamilton, she received her Bachelor's degree in Sociology and Education. Throughout her 30 years as an educator, she has enjoyed teaching students at the elementary, high school and college level. She is a wife to Dominic, a Mamma to three grown children and a Nonna to two incredible granddaughters. Now retired, she dedicates her time to nourishing her passions and interests in cooking, baking, reading, writing and art. She is always up for a creative challenge, which in most cases, consists of family requests that undoubtedly originate in the kitchen.

Taken in 2006 in Ascoli Piceno, the place of my birth, in front of the
original doors of our family's homestead.

Ingram Content Group UK Ltd.
Milton Keynes UK
UKHW051904090323
418254UK00004B/160